CHINA'S EXAMINATION HELL

CHINA'S EXAMINATION HELL

The Civil Service Examinations of Imperial China

by ICHISADA MIYAZAKI

translated by CONRAD SCHIROKAUER

WEATHERHILL *New York & Tokyo*

This book was originally published in Japanese in 1963 by Chūō Kōron-sha under the title Kakyo: Chūgoku no Shiken Jigoku.

First edition, 1976

Published by John Weatherhill, Inc., 149 Madison Avenue, New York, N.Y. 10016, with editorial offices at 7-6-13 Roppongi, Minato-ku, Tokyo 106, Japan. Protected by copyright under terms of the International Copyright Union; all rights reserved. Printed in the Republic of Korea and first published in Japan.

Library of Congress Cataloging in Publication Data: Miyazaki, Ichisada, 1901–/ China's examination hell. / Translation of Kakyo. / Bibliography: p.   / Includes index. / 1. Civil service—China—Examinations. 2. China—Politics and government—1644–1911. / I. Title. / JQ1512. M4813 / 354'.51'003 / 75–16424 / ISBN 0–8348–0104–3

CONTENTS

CONTENTS

INTRODUCTION

EXAMINATIONS! EXAMINATIONS! EXAMINATIONS! All over the world competitive examinations so determine a man's status and career that in many countries practically everyone is involved in one or another examination system sometime in his life. With increasing bureaucratization in both public and private institutions the outlook is for more rather than fewer examinations. Meanwhile, examinations are being scrutinized as never before, and on an international scale, judging by the diversity of nationalities represented by the contributors to the 1969 *World Year Book of Education,* devoted to the subject of examinations.

In this perspective, China's lengthy and well-documented experience merits greater attention than it has received, for many of the problems involved in devising and administering examinations were encountered first by the Chinese. As do all examiners, they labored to keep the tests fair and the testings honest, going to great lengths in their perpetual struggle against cheating, although to the very end the contest of wits remained a draw. The debates over the contents of the examinations, the search for tests that would be both objective and meaningful, the concern with discovering men of high moral character as well as of scholarly and literary attainment are just a few of the large topics inviting comparative analysis.

The Chinese examinations invite comparison, but the Chinese case is unique in that the system of civil service examinations stood alone as the preferred route to success, in contrast to the number of alternative examination systems that are available in most modern countries. In traditional China, government service was by far the most honorable and, in every sense, the most worthwhile occupation; and the examinations played a large part in determining the composition of the elite, by molding as well as selecting the men who operated the political system and dominated the society. Reinforcing a traditional veneration for learning, the examinations gave practical value to education while defining what was to be studied and how

7

the student was to approach his texts. The core of the curriculum was the classics of Confucianism, which, as the state orthodoxy, supplied the moral rationale for the elite and provided all men with a set of personal values while justifying the political structure. It was a rich and varied tradition, which inspired committed scholars, who in turn exhorted their students and disciples to earnest study so that they might seek in the old classics the meaning of life itself. Such teachers constantly deplored the tendency to adopt a careerist attitude toward scholarship, but for the vast majority of men, passing the examinations remained at least the immediate goal.

The examination system further strengthened the ideological principles of both state and society by selecting officials ostensibly on the basis of ability and intellectual achievement rather than of birth. For this reason alone the system was a genuinely pivotal institution. Accordingly, while some familiarity with the Chinese examination system is desirable for the student of comparative education or bureaucracy, it is a necessity for anyone interested in the social and intellectual history of traditional China. Recognition of this fact has led to the production of a solid and growing corpus of scholarly studies upon selected phases and aspects of the examination system, but what has been lacking, at least in English, is a general introduction to the subject for the nonspecialist or the beginning student.

This book provides such an introduction by offering a translation of the only modern scholarly work about the Chinese examination system that has been written for a general audience. Professor Ichisada Miyazaki's audience was Japanese, of course, but except for a foreword and a postscript (omitted from this edition), in which he discussed the Japanese "examination hell," an expression that appeared in his subtitle, his references to specific Japanese institutions or procedures are infrequent and minor.

Having been born in 1901 and raised in a small village in Nagano Prefecture, Professor Miyazaki himself was spared the trials of Japan's "examination hell," partly because education was generously supported in his locality, and partly because in his youth examination competition for entrance into universities was not as intense and widespread as it became after World War II. He studied at Kyoto University and later held the chair of Oriental history there. In his numerous books and other scholarly publications, he has made and continues to make notable contributions to the study of Chinese history, especially in its economic, institutional, and social aspects. He is also well known for his development and refinement of the Naitō thesis, the interpretation of the overall pattern of Chinese history advanced by Naitō Torajirō (1866–1934), Miyazaki's predecessor at Kyoto. A full discussion of these theories would be out of place here, but it is noteworthy that both Naitō and Miyazaki emphasize the importance of the disappearance of China's hereditary aristocracy and its replacement by the literati-bureaucrats who staffed the government from the Sung dynasty (960–1279) down to the demise of the traditional order in our own century. Miyazaki's attention was naturally drawn, therefore, to investigating the history of systems of official recruitment. Upon this subject he has written two other books, one (published in 1956) dealing with the system used before the examination system, and one (published in 1946) concerned with the examination system itself. As Professor Miyazaki has explained in his preface, the book from which this translation has been prepared is not a reworking of that earlier and more technical book but is an entirely new and different account.

Because the examination system left its mark on so many different aspects of Chinese society, it can be studied from a variety of approaches, some of which are suggested in the remarks about sources appended to this translation. In writing the present book, Professor Miyazaki decided to concentrate upon the way the system functioned in its final phase, when it had reached its most complex form, and when much of what earlier had been only implicit in it was fully worked out. One happy consequence of this decision is that it permitted him to draw upon a wide range of source materials, including some of China's novels, short stories, and plays, to illuminate the world of the examinee and bring to life some of the people caught in the meshes of the examination net.

This, then, is not a history of the examination system. And yet Miyazaki never loses sight of the historical perspective that he sketched in his preface and developed in his concluding evaluative chapter. Wisely ignoring what may be called the prehistory of the system—that is, the practice of the Han dynasty (206 B.C–A.D. 221) of testing men recommended to the emperors—Miyazaki places the beginning of the examination system in the attempt by the Sui emperors (589–618) to assert their authority in the face of the old aristocratic families that had dominated China during the preceding period of disunity. When the short-lived Sui dynasty was succeeded by the T'ang (618–906), the examinations were retained by the new regime and again served as a means for broadening the class background of officialdom. But the system did not really flourish until the Sung period, when the old aristocracy no longer existed and rule by civilian bureaucrats was perfected. After that it remained a prominent feature of each new dynasty. The Mongols, in establishing the Yüan dynasty (1271–1368), were slow to reinstitute the examinations but finally did so, after a lapse of forty years; while the Ming emperors

(1368–1644) and the Ch'ing (1644–1911) relied heavily upon it, at the same time neglecting public education. In the meantime, the population growth and an increase in literacy gave rise to the intensification of competition and to the "examination hell" described in this book. Unable to adapt the system to the needs of the modern world, the Ch'ing dynasty abolished it in 1905 as part of a program of reforms that came too late to save either the dynasty or the traditional order itself from collapse six years later. To show what this meant for the unfortunates who had hoped still to achieve careers through the examination system, Miyazaki recounts the plot of a short story by China's greatest modern prose writer, Lu Hsün (1881–1936).

To translate is to choose. Here the attempt has been made to follow the original closely, but not at the expense of the requirements of good English. Also, with the needs of the reader of English in mind, the short bibliography appended to the Japanese edition has been expanded and preceded by a bibliographic essay, and a glossary-index has been added, in the hope that they will be useful both to the general reader and to the student of China's history.

In order to assure accuracy, Miss Sachiko Murakami, who teaches Japanese at the City College of New York, and Mr. Yoneo Nakamura, of the Kyoto Japanese Language School, have carefully checked an early draft of this translation, each having read about half the text. Their help is acknowledged with much gratitude.

The final draft was completed in Kyoto in 1971 and 1972, and owes something to the encouragement and suggestions of compatriots there, especially Peter Golas, Paul Ropp, and Robert Somers, as well as to the help of Professor Hiromichi Takeda, whose daughter, Mrs. Agni Shibata, undertook the onerous task of typing the manuscript. The index was compiled with the thoughtful assistance of Robert Moss of Bergenfield, New Jersey. Without the cheerful support of my wife, Lore, there would have been no manuscript, at least not in English.

This is Professor Miyazaki's book, and now it is time to hear his thoughts.

CONRAD SCHIROKAUER

CHINA'S EXAMINATION HELL

CHAPTER ONE

PREPARING FOR THE EXAMINATIONS

COMPETITION FOR A CHANCE to take the civil service examinations began, if we may be allowed to exaggerate only a little, even before birth. On the back of many a woman's copper mirror the five-character formula "Five Sons Pass the Examinations" expressed her heart's desire to bear five successful sons. Girls, since they could not take the examinations and become officials but merely ran up dowry expenses, were no asset to a family; a man who had no sons was considered to be childless. People said that thieves warned each other not to enter a household with five or more girls because there would be nothing to steal in it. The luckless parents of girls hoped to make up for such misfortune in the generation of their grandchildren by sending their daughters into marriage equipped with those auspicious mirrors.

Prenatal care began as soon as a woman was known to be pregnant. She had to be very careful then, because her conduct was thought to have an influence on the unborn child, and everything she did had to be right. She had to sit erect, with her seat and pillows arranged in exactly the proper way, to sleep without carelessly pillowing her head on an arm, to abstain from strange foods, and so on. She had to be careful to avoid unpleasant colors, and she spent her leisure listening to poetry and the classics being read aloud. These preparations were thought to lead to the birth of an unusually gifted boy.

If, indeed, a boy was born the whole family rejoiced, but if a girl arrived everyone was dejected. On the third day after her birth it was the custom to place a girl on the floor beneath her bed, and to make her grasp a tile and a pebble so that even then she would begin to form a lifelong habit of submission and an acquaintance with hardship. In contrast, in early times when a boy was born arrows were shot from an exorcising bow in the four directions of the compass and straight up and down. In later times, when literary accomplishments had become more important than the martial arts, this

13

practice was replaced by the custom of scattering coins for servants and others to pick up as gifts. Frequently the words "First-place Graduate" were cast on those coins, to signify the highest dream of the family and indeed of the entire clan.

It was thought best for a boy to start upon his studies as early as possible. From the very beginning he was instructed almost entirely in the classics, since mathematics could be left to merchants, while science and technology were relegated to the working class. A potential grand official must study the Four Books, the Five Classics, and other Confucian works, and, further, he must know how to compose poems and write essays. For the most part, questions in civil service examinations did not go beyond these areas of competence.

When he was just a little more than three years old, a boy's education began at home, under the supervision of his mother or some other suitable person. Even at this early stage the child's home environment exerted a great effect upon his development. In cultivated families, where books were stacked high against the walls, the baby sitter taught the boy his first characters while playing. As far as possible these were characters written with only a few strokes.

These twenty-five characters were taught first:

可 佳 八 尔 七 化 孔 上
知 作 九 小 十 三 乙 大
礼 仁 子 生 士 千 己 人
也

Read vertically from right to left, these beginner's characters spelled out an encouraging verse:

> Let us present our work to father.
> Confucius himself
>   taught three thousand.
> Seventy were capable gentlemen.
> You young scholars,
>   eight or nine!
> Work well to attain virtue,
>   and you will understand propriety.

First a character was written in outline with red ink on a single sheet of paper. Then the boy was made to fill it in with black ink. Finally he himself had to write each character. At this stage there was no special need for him to know the meanings of the characters.

After he had learned in this way to hold the brush and to write a number of characters, he usually started on the *Primer of One Thousand Characters*. This is a poem that begins:

Heaven is dark, earth is yellow,
The universe vast and boundless . . .

It consists of a total of two hundred and fifty lines, and since no character is repeated, it provided the student with a foundation of a thousand basic ideograms.

Upon completing the *Primer*, a very bright boy, who could memorize one thing after another without difficulty, would go on to a history text called *Meng Ch'iu* (*The Beginner's Search*) and then proceed to the Four Books and the Five Classics normally studied in school. If rumors of such a prodigy reached the capital, a special "youth examination" was held, but often such a precocious boy merely served as a plaything for adults and did not accomplish much in later life. Youth examinations were popular during the Sung dynasty, but declined and finally were eliminated when people realized how much harm they did to the boys.

Formal education began at about seven years of age (or eight, counting in Chinese style). Boys from families that could afford the expense were sent to a temple, village, communal, or private school staffed by former officials who had lost their positions, or by old scholars who had repeatedly failed the examinations as the years slipped by. Sons of rich men and powerful officials often were taught at home by a family tutor in an elegant small room located in a detached building, which stood in a courtyard planted with trees and shrubs, in order to create an atmosphere conducive to study.

A class usually consisted of eight or nine students. Instruction centered on the Four Books, beginning with the *Analects*, and the process of learning was almost entirely a matter of sheer memorization. With their books open before them, the students would parrot the teacher, phrase by phrase, as he read out the text. Inattentive students, or those who amused themselves by playing with toys hidden in their sleeves, would be scolded by the teacher or hit on the palms and thighs with his fan-shaped "warning ruler." The high regard for discipline was reflected in the saying, "If education is not strict, it shows that the teacher is lazy."

Students who had learned how to read a passage would return to their seats and review what they had just been taught. After reciting it a hundred times, fifty times while looking at the book and fifty with the book face down, even the least gifted would have memorized it. At first the boys were given twenty to thirty characters a day, but as they became more experienced they memorized one, two, or several hundred each day. In order not to force a student beyond his capacity, a boy who could memorize four hundred characters would be assigned no more than two hundred. Otherwise he might become so distressed as to end by detesting his studies.

Along with the literary curriculum, the boys were taught proper conduct, such as when to use honorific terms, how to bow to superiors and to equals, and so forth—although from a modern point of view their training in deportment may seem somewhat defective, as is suggested by the incident concerning a high-ranking Chinese diplomat in the late Ch'ing dynasty who startled Westerners by blowing his nose with his fingers at a public ceremony.

It was usual for a boy to enter school at the age of eight and to complete the general classical education at fifteen. The heart of the curriculum was the classics. If we count the number of characters in the classics that the boys were required to learn by heart, we get the following figures:

Analects	11,705
Mencius	34,685
Book of Changes	24,107
Book of Documents	25,700
Book of Poetry	39,234
Book of Rites	99,010
Tso Chuan	196,845

The total number of characters a student had to learn, then, was 431,286.

The *Great Learning* and the *Doctrine of the Mean,* which together with the *Analects* and the *Mencius* constitute the Four Books, are not counted separately, since they are included in the *Book of Rites.* And, of course, those were not 431,286 *different* characters: most of the ideographs would have been used many times in the several texts. Even so, the task of having to memorize textual material amounting to more than 400,000 characters is enough to make one reel. They required exactly six years of memorizing, at the rate of two hundred characters a day.

After the students had memorized a book, they read commentaries, which often were several times the length of the original text, and practiced answering questions involving passages selected as examination topics. On top of all this, other classical, historical, and literary works had to be scanned, and some literary works had to be examined carefully, since the students were required to write poems and essays modeled upon them. Anyone not very vigorous mentally might well become sick of it all halfway through the course.

Moreover, the boys were at an age when the urge to play is strongest, and they suffered bitterly when they were confined all day in a classroom as though under detention. Parents and teachers, therefore, supported a lad, urging him on to "become a great man!" From ancient times, many poems were composed on the theme, "If you study while young, you will get ahead." The Sung emperor Chentsung wrote such a one:

> To enrich your family, no need to buy good land:
> Books hold a thousand measures of grain.
> For an easy life, no need to build a mansion:
> In books are found houses of gold.
> Going out, be not vexed at absence of followers:
> In books, carriages and horses form a crowd.
> Marrying, be not vexed by lack of a good go-between:
> In books there are girls with faces of jade.
> A boy who wants to become a somebody
> Devotes himself to the classics, faces the window, and reads.

In later times this poem was criticized because it tempted students with the promise of beautiful women and riches, but that was the very reason it was effective.

Nonetheless, in all times and places students find shortcuts to learning. Despite repeated official and private injunctions to study the Four Books and Five Classics honestly, rapid-study methods were devised with the sole purpose of preparing candidates for the examinations. Because not very many places in the classics were suitable as subjects for examination questions, similar passages and problems were often repeated. Aware of this, publishers compiled collections of examination answers, and a candidate who, relying on these compilations, guessed successfully during the course of his own examination could obtain a good rating without having worked very hard. But if he guessed wrong he faced unmitigated disaster because, unprepared, he would have submitted so bad a paper that the officials could only shake their heads and fail him. Reports from perturbed officials caused the government to issue frequent prohibitions of the publication of such collections of model answers, but since it was a profitable business with a steady demand, ways of issuing them surreptitiously were arranged, and time and again the prohibitions rapidly became mere empty formalities.

CHAPTER TWO

THE DISTRICT AND PREFECTURAL
EXAMINATIONS

DURING ITS LONG HISTORY of almost fourteen hundred years, the Chinese examination system underwent many changes, and by the time the Ch'ing dynasty came to power it had developed into something quite different from what it had been at the start. Rather than attempt a complete survey here, it seems better to describe the system as it was about a hundred years ago, near the end of the Ch'ing dynasty, when it had reached its greatest complexity.

The system consisted of series of difficult examinations, which can be divided into two groups: school entrance examinations and civil service examinations proper. Actually, the school entrance examinations were not intended originally as part of the examination system but were added to it during the Ming dynasty to serve as preparatory tests prior to the civil service examinations. Ever since the Ming period, entrance to the latter was limited to men with student status, that is, to *sheng-yüan*, or licentiates; and those who wished to take the civil service examinations had to acquire that status first by passing an entrance examination for a government school. The Ch'ing officials simply continued the Ming system, only making the examinations more difficult.

At that time, the government school system consisted of a national university in the capital, and prefectural (*fu*), departmental (*chou*), and district (*hsien*) schools in the provinces. Although they differed in such matters as the salaries and ranks of their staffs, the prefectural, departmental, and district schools were on the same level as far as instruction was concerned, and their licentiates were equal in status. All students had to pass what were commonly called the "youth examinations," held twice during every three-year period. These consisted of (1) the district examination (*hsien-shih*), conducted by the district; (2) the prefectural examination (*fu-shih*), held by the prefecture; and (3) the qualifying examination (*yüan-shih*), which may be called the final examination, administered by the provincial director of studies (*hsüeh-cheng*) in the prefectural capital.

There were a few restrictions on admission to the examinations. One stipulated that for the past three generations a candidate's family had not engaged in a "base occupation," such as running a brothel, and a candidate needed a guarantor to certify that in this respect his family was unsullied. Otherwise there were no class restrictions: a student was not asked whether he was a merchant, artisan, or peasant, nor did he receive any special privileges if his ancestors had been gentlemen, that is, officials. A man in mourning for a parent or grandparent was excluded from the examinations, since a regulation provided that he could not undertake any official affairs during the one to three years he must spend in mourning.

Upon his application form the candidate had to indicate that these restrictions did not apply to him, and he filled in the spaces provided for his age, state of health, and special physical features. Since photography did not yet exist, he had to indicate whether he was short or tall, dark or pale in complexion, and whether he wore a beard.

Although there was no age limit on admission to these "youth examinations," originally they had been intended for youngsters who had not yet undergone the capping ceremony that marked a boy's coming of age in his fifteenth year. Therefore, uncapped youths were favored by receiving easy questions, and their answers were graded leniently, while older candidates were discriminated against and made to write upon difficult questions, the answers to which were graded severely. As a result, almost every applicant gave a false age. At the worst, men forty or fifty years of age shaved off their beards and took the examinations, claiming that they were boys of fourteen. Faced with an almost universal abuse of their good nature, and not knowing where to draw the line, officials would obligingly overlook the lines on an older man's face. There are humorous stories about the elderly wife of such an old candidate not recognizing him when he came home after shaving his beard for the examination, and trying to turn him out of the house as she asked, "Whose child are you?" Since such absurd falsifications of age depended upon the sympathy of the authorities, the extent of the practice differed from place to place.

The district examination was given in a spacious examination hall or shed, a *k'ao-p'eng,* attached to the district office, or yamen. To prevent shady dealings and to guard against suspicions of collusion, the magistrate cut off all communication with the outside world from the time the candidates entered the *k'ao-p'eng* until the examination was over.

At about three or four o'clock in the morning of the examination day, well before dawn, a cannon shot sounded with a deafening roar.

That was the signal for the students billeted in different parts of the city to rise and prepare themselves. An hour or an hour and a half later, there was a second shot, at which the candidates left their quarters to go to the examination hall. With each one carrying in a basket everything needed for the examination—an inkstone as flat and light as possible, a first-class ink stick, brushes, lunch, water, and the like—they assembled before the gates of the *k'ao-p'eng*. Soon, at the third sounding of the cannon, the great doors were opened on the left and on the right, and the candidates, along with fathers, brothers, and friends, surged in a crowd into the hall. Each candidate then looked for his desk, indicated by a numbered tally stick.

At a signal, all those people accompanying the candidates had to leave. Now, with the candidates sitting alone at their desks, the hall became as silent as a tomb, and instantly a gloomy atmosphere prevailed. Then the magistrate appeared, in ceremonial dress, together with the teachers from the district school and their students, the local licentiates. When he heard his name called, each candidate came forward and bowed to the magistrate. A licentiate acting as his guarantor then confirmed the identity of the candidate, who took a set of answer sheets and returned to his seat. These answer sheets (*shih-chuan*) were in the form of a folded book of plain white paper with ruled lines printed in red.

When the distribution of answer sheets was completed, the guarantors left the hall, and the magistrate himself went to lock the entrance with a key and affixed a seal upon it. After all these preliminary activities, the hour of seven had been reached. Resuming his seat, the magistrate announced the first question. It was written out on a large piece of paper pasted upon a placard (*pang*) and carried around the hall so that everyone might read it.

This first question was taken from the Four Books. If, for example, the passage in the *Analects* was selected that reads, "There are three things a gentleman fears," the candidate would write an essay quoting the next passage, "He fears the will of heaven, he fears great men, he fears the words of the sages," add the view of Chu Hsi, and conclude with his own explanation.

As has been indicated, there were different questions for uncapped youths and for capped candidates, with the latter being subjected to very difficult questions. Indeed, to prevent someone from passing just because he had happened to prepare the right passage, the examiners sometimes posed questions so dreadfully distorted as to make them almost impossible to understand. For example, questions might be asked concerning the circle placed above "the Master said" in the *Analects* and other classics; or, again, the candidates would be asked to name the one place in the *Analects* where the three particles *yeh, chi,* and *i* occur in sequence. When the examiners saw that no one could answer such a question, they happily called out, "We have outwitted them."

An hour after the first question had been announced, the proctors went around and stamped a seal on the papers to indicate how far each student had progressed in his answer. An average candidate was expected to have written a few lines by then. If a man had not written anything at all, and the stamp appeared at the very beginning of his paper, he would not receive a high grade even if thereafter he managed to compose a good answer, because there was always the suspicion that he had cribbed it from someone else.

Between nine and ten o'clock, the rest of the examination was given out. This consisted of two questions: another one based upon the Four Books, and one requiring the candidates to compose a poem, using five words to a line, on a set theme and to a set rhyme. The candidates worked on their answers until evening. When it became too dark to write, they were not allowed to light candles but had to turn in their papers whether or not they were finished. They were not permitted to leave individually but were let out in groups of fifty, the doors being locked after each group's departure to prevent unauthorized persons from entering the hall.

For three or four days after this first examination session, the magistrate, bearing sole responsibility, had to work day and night judging the papers. Some magistrates, however, such as former military officers who had been rewarded with a civilian post, could not themselves do this literary work, and sought help from private secretaries (*mu-yu*) or instructors at a neighboring private academy. Such readers, as well as the magistrate himself, were not permitted to set foot outside the examination hall until the last paper was graded. Furthermore, to prevent irregularities, the names on the answer sheets were covered (*hu-ming*), so that only the seat number was visible during grading. If many candidates wrote almost identical answers echoing each other, and there was no doubt that they had crammed from a collection of model answers, such as was prohibited by the imperial court, all were failed for "recopying" (*lui-t'ung*). Frequently, substitutes took the examinations in place of candidates, and readers could not discover this deception from the papers alone. But if they received secret information, or found out about the substitution by checking the handwriting, they imposed a heavy penalty. Similarly, a magistrate who took a bribe or showed favoritism was punished most severely: he lost his office immediately and might even be banished.

Candidates who discovered a mistake in an examination question were permitted to report it quietly; but if many of them raised a fuss and staged a mass walkout from the hall, they were condemned for striking. The ringleaders were punished, and all examinations in the prefecture were canceled, thus not only disgracing the area but also affecting all future candidates for an indefinite period.

When the grading of the answer sheets was finished, the results were announced. The dramatic production the authorities made of this important event was a special feature of the system. For the district examinations the names of successful candidates were written on sheets of paper large enough to hold fifty names. The name of the best candidate was placed at the top, in the twelve o'clock position, and the names of the rest were written counterclockwise, in order of descending rank. Then the men in charge checked each name with a mark in black ink, distinguished it with a red dot, wrote "successful" (*chung*) in the empty space at the center of the list, and, lining up all the sheets, posted them in front of the yamen gates. In consequence of this elaborate procedure, the successful candidates were all the more exalted, while the failures became more and more despondent.

This public posting of the results in such a grand manner was, in part, a measure taken for the protection of the examiners, a way of indicating that everything about the test had been open and fair. Yet sometimes it did happen that, as soon as the names were announced, there was a great outcry against the results. Inasmuch as this occurred despite the elaborate public announcement, there is no telling what difficulties the officials might have encountered had they informed the candidates privately. Because everyone followed the examination results with the greatest interest, tempers were strained at all levels, and examinees and examiners alike were under great pressure. Since officials were content as long as there were no serious errors and their fairness was not challenged, and since candidates feared that they would fail if they wrote something too different from the run-of-the-mill sorts of answers, both groups stifled any tendencies toward originality. The real purpose of the examinations—to select men who would be of greatest service to the country in the future—was lost.

The announcement of the results of the first session did not conclude the district examination. On the day after this announcement a second examination was held, consisting of three parts: one based upon the Four Books, one upon the Five Classics, and the third requiring the composition of a poem. This time no distinction was made between the capped and the uncapped candidates. But the first test was the most important, and only a few candidates were eliminated in the second and subsequent sessions. A day after the results of the second test were made public, the third examination took place. This consisted of a topic from the Four Books, a poem, and a piece of rhymed prose in the *fu* style. A day after the results of this examination were announced, the fourth session was held. This time candidates had to answer a question from the Four Books, compose a poem, and write an essay, usually concerned with historical events or government.

The fifth test, also known as the final examination, was mostly a matter of form, and the custom was not to fail anyone who took it. Once again there was a question from the Four Books, but all that the candidates had to do was to write the first few sentences of a possible answer. The most important part was to write down, without making a mistake, one of the sixteen articles of the *Sheng-lun Kuang-hsün*. This may rightly be called an Imperial Rescript on Education, and was issued by the fifth emperor of the Ch'ing dynasty, Yung-cheng (r. 1723–36). In China this kind of pronouncement on education began with Emperor T'ai-tsu of the Ming dynasty (r. 1368–99), who issued the *Sheng-lun Liu-yen* for the moral edification of his people:

> Do your duty to your parents.
> Honor your elders.
> Be at peace with your neighbors.
> Instruct sons and grandsons.
> Be content in your occupation.
> Do not commit offenses.

In the Ch'ing period, Emperor K'ang-hsi (r. 1662–1723) expanded this to sixteen articles. His son, Yung-cheng, further enlarged it to ten thousand words, and gave it the title *Sheng-lun Kuang-hsün*. In time it became the practice to require that one of the articles be reproduced verbatim by candidates in the last session of the district, prefectural, and qualifying examinations.

The *Sheng-lun Kuang-hsün* reached Japan during the Tokugawa period (1603–1868). Its persistent influence on Japanese thought can be seen in Emperor Meiji's Imperial Rescript on Education, issued in 1890, and in his Precepts to Soldiers and Sailors, proclaimed in 1882, which is even closer in style to the Chinese medel.

Because the *Sheng-lun Kuang-hsün* was written by an emperor, it had to be reproduced without a single mistake, for an error was considered to be a grave act of *lèse-majesté*. A candidate guilty of this transgression was failed no matter how good the rest of his paper was, and he might even be barred from participating in a number of subsequent examinations. Moreover, candidates had to be certain to avoid the characters used in writing an emperor's name. This taboo applied not only to the reigning emperor but also to all his predecessors from the same dynasty. Therefore other characters identical in pronunciation were substituted for those preempted by the imperial names. Aside from these details, the text of the *Sheng-lun Kuang-hsün* presented few problems to men who had already memorized the Four Books and Five Classics, although it would be a severe strain on people like ourselves who have not undergone such rigorous training. Furthermore, having been successful so far, the candidates were in a good frame of mind to surmount this final obstacle.

By this time the magistrate had become fond of the candidates, and it was customary for him to invite them to dinner on the evening of the day the final session was completed. This banquet also celebrated the magistrate's own pleasure at completing the greater part of one of his most important duties. At this feast, held in the examination hall, eight dishes were served to each table of eight guests. At the end of the banquet the candidates congratulated the examination staff.

After reading the fifth set of examination papers, the magistrate's final task was to determine for each candidate the average of the grades from all of his examinations and to announce the names of the successful candidates in the same manner as before. After that the magistrate, who had been confined to the examination hall for about twenty days, could return to his official quarters and relax. But he was not yet free from care, for he was responsible in part for the scholarship of the men he had passed until they completed the next stage, the prefectural examination. Here, in order to save the face of the magistrate, those whom he had ranked at the top were seldom failed. But sometimes it did happen that the top-ranking candidate made too many mistakes, or that others submitted papers that were too much below the level of expectation, and then the magistrate was blamed and punished.

No generalization can be made about the intensity of competition among students during the district examination, since this varied from place to place. As a preliminary test, the district examination was intended to eliminate as many candidates as possible and to pass only the number that would be close to the final school quota. In very general terms, about four times the number of candidates wanted in the final quota were passed in the district examinations; half of these were retained in the prefectural examination; and again half of these were passed in the qualifying examination. But in some places ten times as many candidates took the examinations as there were openings for, and in others almost everyone was passed. The quota for each district school was decided on the basis of the cultural level and population of the area, and the quotas ranged from a maximum of twenty-five to a minimum of three or four. Thus, in cities, where the cultural level was high, competition was intense, while in remoter places an able boy's chance to enter school was comparatively easy. Since, however, all candidates faced a series of difficult examinations in the future, it was an advantage for them to experience severe competition from the very start of their education.

The district examination was difficult enough, but it was merely the beginning of the beginning. The only privilege granted those who passed it was permission to take the prefectural examination. District examinations themselves were scheduled to enable those who passed them to participate in prefectural examinations; and they were given at the same time in each district in order to prevent a man from lying about his permanent domicile and taking the examination twice.

Prefectural examinations were conducted by the prefect in the prefectural capital, quite a large bustling city with a permanent examination hall (*shih-yüan*). On the day of the examination, the candidates gathered early in the morning in front of the hall and, grouped by districts, entered the *shih-yüan,* led by teachers from the district schools. Again the examination was administered in three parts. The procedures were identical with those of the district examination, including the reproducing of an article from the *Sheng-lun Kuang-hsün* during the third and last session, and even the banquet when the ordeal was ended.

This was a significant second testing of those who had passed earlier: it determined whether their scholarship was adequate for taking the next examination and eliminated about half of the candidates at this stage. Each group was given a different set of questions, and the decision about who should be passed was made separately for each district. The announcement of the successful candidates was made just as in the district examination, except that now the fifty names on each sheet were arranged clockwise.

CHAPTER THREE

THE QUALIFYING EXAMINATION

THE QUALIFYING EXAMINATION was given soon after the results of the prefectural examination were announced, although the exact date depended on the time at which the provincial director of studies reached the prefecture. This official ranked below the governor general and governor, the highest provincial officials during Ch'ing times, but he certainly was not their subordinate. In keeping with the high importance attached to learning, educational matters were separated from other administrative concerns. The director of studies was responsible directly to the emperor and could complain to him if he thought that the governor general or governor had done something unsuitable. Furthermore, after his three-year tour of duty in a province, he was received by the emperor in a personal audience and reported upon conditions in the province quite apart from educational matters. Thus, the governor general and governor, with all their local power, still had to treat the director of studies as an equal.

The director of studies' duties were not primarily administrative, since most such tasks were handled by the prefects and magistrates under his general supervision. His main responsibility was that of an examination official: it was his duty to visit each of the ten or so prefectures in the province twice during his three-year tour, once for the "annual" examination (discussed in the next chapter) and once for the special preliminary examination (*k'o-shih*) given to test the qualifications of licentiates who wished to take the civil service examinations. The qualifying examination, held at the same time, actually was the most important of the three, because it was the last school-entrance examination leading to the rank of licentiate.

The director's tour schedule determined the dates for the prefectural and district examinations. When the director arrived in a city, he was met by its prefect and escorted to a residence near the examination hall. During the next day he paid his respects at the local temple of Confucius and convened the students for a lecture on the classics. Several days later the examination began. On the day before that, the director entered the examination compound and shut himself off completely from the outside world, just as the examiners for lesser tests had done. Since the director had no immediate subordinates to assist him, other than his private secretaries, the duties of administering the examination were assigned to the prefect.

Early in the morning of the day the examination began, there was a great congestion, as not only the candidates but also the magistrates of each district, the staffs of the district schools, the licentiates, and others gathered in front of the large portals of the examination hall. When the gates opened at the third cannon shot, the candidates, grouped by district, streamed through and lined up at the second gate (*i-men*), where the prefectural clerks searched them "back and front," looking for reference books, notes, ponies, or money with which they might bribe a clerk. If something proscribed was found, the inspecting clerk received an award and the candidate was punished. After the inspection the candidates went through the door in groups of about twenty and entered the examination room, passing in front of the prefect, to whom they bowed. At this point the identity of the candidates was authenticated by their guarantors. Then the candidates received their answer papers and went to their designated seats in the large and spacious hall, capable of accommodating a thousand men at a time. On the cover of each set of answer sheets was pasted a small label, on which three seals had been stamped where it joined the cover. Each candidate wrote his name on the label, tore it off, and kept it. From then until the end of the examination a candidate's name was kept secret, and only his seat number was used to identify him and his answer.

By the time everyone had reached his seat it was day. The first query concerned the Four Books. A different question for candidates from each district was stuck on a placard and circulated in the appropriate area of the hall. After two hours a second question relating to the Four Books was announced, and a poem on a given theme was assigned. The candidates had until evening to complete their answers.

Since this was the last school entrance examination, it had to be conducted most strictly; and since so many candidates were gathered in one place, officials had to preserve silence and prevent irregularities. To this effect, the director of studies prepared ten different seals. When a clerk saw a candidate doing something improper he immediately went to his place and stamped the appropriate seal on his paper. The ten seals read:

1. *Leaving one's seat.* (A candidate was allowed to leave his seat

only once, to drink tea or go to the toilet. When he did so he had to leave his answer sheet with a clerk and retrieve it when he returned to the hall. Because going to the toilet was a troublesome and time-consuming procedure, most candidates brought a pot, which they placed under their seat, and used that.)

2. *Exchanging papers.* (If students traded papers they were suspected of conspiring to have the better scholar write an answer for the other.)
3. *Dropping a paper.* (This was indiscreet because it aroused suspicion about exchanging papers.)
4. *Talking.*
5. *Gazing around and looking at others' papers.*
6. *Changing seats.* (Slipping into another's empty seat.)
7. *Disobeying.* (Failing to comply with clerks' instructions.)
8. *Violating regulations.*
9. *Humming.* (This often happened when candidates were preparing rhymes for poems, and was a great annoyance to others.)
10. *Incomplete.* (When a paper was not finished by sunset this seal was stamped upon it, lest someone add to it later.)

One such stamp upon a paper did not necessarily prove that something was wrong, but it seriously affected the judge's impression and meant certain failure, since many fine papers without a stamp were submitted. Another cause for instant failure was disorderly or illegible calligraphy, because the characters had to be written in the square style, with the brushstrokes correctly placed in the four corners. Otherwise, no matter how good the content of the paper was, it would be passed over, with the examiners barely glancing at it.

About one or two o'clock in the afternoon the clerks called out in loud voices, "Quickly complete your clean copies," and around three or four o'clock they called out, "Quickly submit your papers." Thereupon each candidate rapidly checked his answers, made certain that he possessed the name slip torn from the cover of the answer sheets, handed in his papers, and received an exit pass. This was a bamboo tally, which he threw into a basket placed beside the inner gate. At the great outer gate he had to wait until fifty men had assembled, whereupon it was opened and they were permitted to leave in a group.

The first group left about three or four o'clock, to the accompaniment of three cannon shots. Those who remained continued to work upon their papers, and a second group left about an hour later. The last departure took place at five o'clock. If someone was still lingering in his seat at that time, an official would come and stamp "Incomplete" upon his paper before taking it away.

When all the papers were gathered in, the director of studies hurried to inspect them. He was assisted by his private secretaries, of whom there were five or six for a small province, while for a large one there might be more than ten. Since they were well acquainted with the ideas of the director, they selected answers that would please him in style and content. The candidates, too, studied the writings of the director before they took the examination, and composed answers conforming with his views. Thus, in the short three years of his tour the director exercised great influence upon local scholarship: he held the "handles of literature," as people said, meaning that he controlled the direction of culture.

Two days after the examination, the results were announced by seat number. Generally, the number of candidates who were passed was about thirty percent higher than the school quota allowed, although sometimes it was as high as fifty percent. On the afternoon of that day or the morning of the next, the second session was held. The candidates again used their former seats and wrote only the seat numbers upon their answer sheets. After another day the results were announced. This time the school quota was not exceeded, and the final selections were just about made. In addition to those who qualified for entrance into the district schools, the better candidates were chosen for admission to the prefectural school. Also a certain number of "reserve" men (*i-sheng,* or, more colloquially, *han-ko hsiu-ts'ai,* that is, apprentice scholars) were selected to skip the next district and prefectural examinations, thereby receiving priority for taking the qualifying examination again.

However, the qualifying examination was not yet finished, for again there were two further sessions. As part of the third session, in addition to answering questions relating to the interpretation of the classics, the candidates had to write from memory the first few sentences of their answer for the first examination paper. This served as a double check on the identity of the candidates, who were required also to produce the name slips they had saved from the first examination. Usually, none failed this third examination, nor the fourth, which tied things together. In this last formal session, once again there were themes from the Four Books and the Five Classics and a poetry assignment, but no stress was placed upon the results, and the candidates were required only to write out a passage from the *Sheng-lun Kuang-hsün.* In the interval, the director of studies used the time to go through the candidates' papers from earlier district and prefectural examinations in order to verify the calligraphy. Only when this was completed could the results be announced. The actual responsibility for this announcement was the prefect's, with the director of studies merely giving recognition to the candidates' attainments in scholarship.

Those who had been successful were entitled now to enter their respective schools, but it was the prefect in his capacity as chief local administrator who had the authority to admit students to these schools. The announcement of those who had passed also served as a school-entrance ceremony, and was carried out according to an exact routine prescribed by Chinese bureaucratic practice.

On the day of this important event, the prefect, dressed in his ceremonial robes and accompanied by attendants, left his yamen in a palanquin, to the accompaniment of three rounds of cannon, and proceeded to the prefectural school while musicians played. Another three rounds of cannon were fired while the prefect descended from his palanquin and made his way to a platform inside the temple of Confucius located within the school compound. These cannon shots were the signal for posting the examination results in the great hall of the temple, a location chosen to symbolize the fact that entrance into a national school was equivalent to formally becoming a disciple of Confucius. Upon this occasion, the prefect announced to Confucius the entrance of new disciples into the school.

The director of studies and successful candidates did not take part in this ceremony, but stayed in their residences. Then the new *sheng-yüan,* proud of their status, escorted by the staff members of their schools, called upon the director to express their gratitude for being passed. This was their first opportunity to wear the uniform prescribed for a licentiate: a dark blue garment bordered in black and a "sparrow top" cap. The director had an audience with each new *sheng-yüan* and gave him a cap ornament of gold foil attached to red paper, known as a "gold flower." As the *sheng-yüan* reverently raised this insignia of the new matriculant to his head and fixed it to his cap, his spirit rejoiced.

Next, the names of those who had passed were reported to their districts. Each man's name was written upon a great piece of red paper decorated with flowers around its edges, which had been prepared in advance in the district school. Now this "victory announcement" (*chieh-pao*) was delivered to the man's home. It was only a notice of admission, but instead of merely sending something like a postcard, the Chinese issued a dramatic and courteous invitation:

VICTORY ANNOUNCEMENT
This School Gives Notice—May He Come In First
For Three Degrees in a Row

Your Honorable Son-in-law CHANG HSÜN-HUA
By order of Magistrate Lu of Chiang-ning District, holding
the brevet rank of Coadministrator and temporarily acting
for the Magistrate of Shanghai District under Sung-chiang
Prefecture, Kiangsu Province, is to select an auspicious day
for entry into the district school to begin his studies.

The expression "three degrees in a row" referred to the three tests
that the licentiate would take in the future, the provincial, metropolitan, and palace examinations. Thus, these are really words of
congratulation, conveying the polite wish that he will come in first
in all three events. As is indicated by its literal meaning, "victory
announcement" originally was a military term signifying success in
battle. After the examination system became predominant, other
military terms too were applied verbatim to the examinations. In-
stances are plentiful: "successive victories in successive battles,"
"successive battles without success," "hard fighting on three battle-
fields," "the general of a defeated army does not discuss military
matters," or, even more ironically, "a brave general of a thousand
armies and ten thousand horses."

When the messenger from the prefectural school arrived at the
residence of a successful candidate and shouted, "Congratulations on
your success," the delighted family gave him a handsome tip, even
if the candidate himself had not yet returned home. It is said that,
with this in mind, some of the messengers reported congratulations
to every hopeful family. Since the "victory announcement" was
mounted like a scroll, it was displayed prominently in the house,
where it could be admired by a steady stream of friends and relatives
come to express their felicitations.

After the new licentiates returned to their districts, the school-
entrance ceremonies took place. The magistrate, accompanied by
the instructors, called them together in the district school's temple of
Confucius and had them do homage to the statue of Confucius and
take again the oath making them his disciples. After the ceremony,
it was customary for the instructors to invite the new licentiates to a
dinner. The *sheng-yüan*, in their turn, celebrated with a banquet to
which they invited friends and relatives. Sometimes, too, they
printed and distributed their own examination answers. It was also
the custom for the guests to arrive with appropriate congratulatory
gifts. In addition, the new *sheng-yüan* presented an entrance fee to
their instructors and gifts of money to thank the senior licentiates who
had served as their guarantors. Inasmuch as the rich set the standards of generosity in those matters, the expenses involved in reaching
sheng-yüan status were so great that, from the start, it was impossible

for sons of the poor to enter school. In education, as in all else, a class distinction was established that was based upon wealth, with the rich constantly becoming richer, while the poor had to resign themselves to remaining forever at the bottom of society.

CHAPTER FOUR

THE "ANNUAL" AND SPECIAL PRELIMINARY EXAMINATIONS

ORIGINALLY THE SCHOOL SYSTEM and the examination system were separate and distinct. Schools were intended for educating students, and those young men who had studied for a long time and taken many examinations were given an opportunity to become officials directly without entering the competitive examination system. As time went on, however, the distinction between the pedagogic and the examining institutions was lost. Since status as a *sheng-yüan* was a prerequisite for taking the civil service examinations, men came to consider the school-entrance examinations that conveyed this status as merely the first stage in the examination system. This trend was intensified when the government created a whole series of entrance examinations as a way of dealing with the many aspirants to office and of eliminating those who were deemed to be superfluous.

Yet the original school system continued to exist as before, and the "annual" examinations began as tests of scholarship in accordance with the pedagogic functions of the schools. But gradually, precisely because they were academic and not career examinations, people managed to disregard them. To understand how this happened, let us look at the schools themselves.

School enrollment was of two kinds. First, there were the regular students, divided into stipend students (*lin-sheng*) and extra students (*tseng-sheng*). Originally the number of licentiates had been limited to a maximum of forty for a large school and to about fifteen for small schools, and each student had been provided with a government allowance. However, in the face of pressure for the creation of more licentiates, the government decided to permit a certain number of young men to enter school without stipends, as "extra students." Their number was almost as great as that of the stipend students. In both cases the quota was strictly limited, and it was impossible to admit a new man unless a vacancy had been created, for instance by death or upon promotion to the imperial university.

Pressed by the increasingly strong desire of prominent people to launch their sons upon an official career, the government finally expanded the number of licentiates by selecting "secondary students" (*fu-sheng*) twice every three years. At the time of each departmental examination the number of men to be admitted into this category was decided, but without fixing a predetermined enrollment quota. All licentiates entered the school system as "secondary students"; and if, later, some were promoted to regular student status, or even if some died, the vacancies so created were not filled, nor was the admissions quota raised.

While in this manner the number of students in the school system swelled until it became immense, the school faculty remained limited to two or three men holding the rank of professor (*chiao-shou*), lecturer (*chiao-yu*), or instructor (*hsün-yao*). Thus, educational supervision of the licentiates necessarily left much to be desired. Faced with an impossible task, the faculty, too, decided to make a good thing of it, became lazy in their own studies, and neglected their teaching duties. The *sheng-yüan*, in turn, did not depend on the instructors but relied on themselves if they really wanted to study. They did not respect the badly treated and frequently unqualified faculty men. All the promising students who did well in the examinations became government administrators, while only the incompetent and inadequate were relegated to the schools, along with men who passed through the examination system at an advanced age or broke down in the middle of the examination sequence. Consequently, administrative officials paid hardly any attention to the school faculty.

The rule of avoidance, which prohibited officials from serving in their home areas, did not apply to a school's faculty. This did not mean that they received preferential treatment, but reflected, rather, the insignificance of those teachers, who, lacking any authority whatsoever, could hardly do any harm even if they served in their native place, surrounded and influenced by relatives. Even at the examinations the faculty had no substantive duties to perform, but merely followed the much younger prefect and had nothing to do but hang around, although they would be berated by the director of studies if the results were uniformly bad. For such men there was almost no hope for an official career: once a man joined a school staff, he had to be satisfied with a miserable salary for the rest of his life.

The licentiates, it should be remembered, were legally students, and as such were required, in theory, to take the annual examination, which originally was a school examination. As has been indicated, it was conducted by the director of studies during his tour of the prefectures, and was given to all licentiates regardless of status. Those who did well were promoted, with secondary students becoming extra students, those rising to become stipend students, and the latter winning admission to the university in the capital.

The annual examination consisted of one question based upon the Four Books, one upon the Five Classics, and one upon the *Book of Poetry*, followed by the writing of a section from the Imperial Rescript of Yung-cheng, the *Sheng-lun Kuang-hsün*. The session lasted one day. The results were divided into six grades, with the first two constituting the top rank (*yu-teng*), the next two the middle rank (*chung-teng*), and the last two the lowest rank (*lieh-teng*). Those candidates achieving top rank were promoted, and secondary students who finished in the first grade received stipend-student status, provided there was a vacancy. Otherwise they, together with those who had been assigned to the second grade, were promoted to extra-student status, again provided there was a vacancy. Middle-ranked students remained as they were; but those in the two lowest grades were punished with demotion. A secondary student who finished in the fifth category was "demoted to the black cloth" (*ch'ing-i*), that is, suspended; if he finished in the last rank he was dropped from the school, with permission to return later (*fa-she*). If in the next examination he ended again in the lowest rank, he was expelled from school, deprived of his student status, and reduced to the position of an ordinary commoner.

In theory, stipend students after ten years were promoted to the central university on the recommendation of the director of studies. Since such recommendations generally were made in order of seniority, this process could take more than twenty years, although the director could, and frequently did, make exceptions for those *sheng-yüan* who had excelled in the annual examination. Men who in this way became university students retained the privilege of participating in the examination system but also had an opportunity to begin an official career on the basis of grades obtained in university examinations. It was this route from local school to national university and ultimately to officialdom that originally had given the school system its meaning; and the director's original duty had been to supervise local schools and recommend outstanding men from them for admission to the university. But the chances of advancing from the university to officialdom became slight, and to obtain a desirable administrative post was still more difficult. Though some men ended up wasting their youth and waiting in vain, most licentiates, whether assigned to a local school or selected for the national university, concentrated on studying for the civil service examinations and forgot about the alternative route to office through the school system. The government, too, neglected the school system and eventually emphasized the selection of men through the civil service examinations; as a result, the director of studies concentrated his attention upon the departmental examinations and neglected the annual examinations that originally had been his major responsibility.

For the licentiates, too, the annual examination offered the promise neither of excitement nor of glamour, since even a man with an excellent score might have a long wait for promotion and because those who were fortunate enough to become university students were not received with open arms by the world but were treated by the central government like surplus personnel.

Consequently, this examination was considered a waste of time. Alarmed by this trend, the government made it a rule that if someone missed three consecutive examinations his status as a *sheng-yüan* would be revoked. The licentiates interpreted this to mean that they were free to miss two sessions in a row by pretending illness. Since the annual examinations were given only once every three years, licentiates could manage to sit for an examination only once every nine years.

Similar to this shunning of the annual examinations was the tendency of most men to be satisfied with a licentiate's status and to neglect attending the unappealing schools run by a few senile scholars, themselves good examples of examination system stragglers. Scarcely any lectures were given. Even if there were, what did those muddle-headed and out-of-date teachers know about modern trends in scholarship?

Most of the responsibility for the development of this state of affairs lay with the government. Education costs money. Government officials forgot the original purpose of establishing schools, left unchanged the school facilities as well as the size and treatment of their staffs, and increased only the number of students. It was unreasonable to expect such schools to educate men; nor was their failure to do so a cause of official distress, since the civil service examinations drew more than enough candidates for public office. Far from there being a shortage of officials, there was a serious surplus of them, so that it was difficult to find posts for all. Furthermore, giving examinations at intervals was much cheaper than providing proper schooling continuously. That, in practice, was left to the people themselves.

The *sheng-yüan* was no longer a boy but an adult gentleman. Dressed in his special uniform with a cap denoting the lowest rank in civil service, the ninth, he was not yet an official but was treated like one. Ordinary people made way for him in the street, and wherever they gathered he was conducted to the seat of honor even though white-haired old men might be present. If a commoner was discourteous to a *sheng-yüan,* he was subject to prosecution for the crime of contempt for officials. Even if a licentiate was suspected of having committed a crime, the authorities could not arrest him without first obtaining the concurrence of the school staff. Licentiates resembled cadets in the old Japanese army: "Noncommissioned officers, dreaded until yesterday, today salute from afar."

At the same time, *sheng-yüan* were not supposed to do anything to damage their reputations. Although enjoying free access to the official world and able to deal with officials as equals, they were strictly forbidden to involve themselves in lawsuits, like petty lawyers, or use their status to evade paying taxes. They had to be especially careful not to criticize the government or to comment upon political affairs; and, unlike peasants, artisans, and merchants, all of whom were mere commoners, they could not approach the government as practitioners of a recognized occupation. As students they were supposed to concentrate upon their studies and not engage in any profession.

Yet *sheng-yüan,* too, had to make a living. Men from rich families could go on for years and decades studying for the difficult civil service examinations, but those from middle-level families could not afford to be unemployed forever. Luckily, they could find work resembling that of an official by joining the staff of an official as a secretary or associate. Several thousand local clerks were employed in a Chinese government office, or yamen, but because they were notoriously corrupt and untrustworthy, high officials engaged private secretaries as a kind of brain trust. The number of these secretaries ranged from a few men, in the case of a minor local official, to several dozen for a high official. Licentiates, therefore, hunted up connections in an effort to obtain employment on the staffs of administrators with the greatest promise of future influence and success. Inasmuch as their compensation came from the pocket money of their employer, their income was not high, but it was enough to support a family. In some cases, when jobs that had begun as sidelines became their main occupations, unambitious men lost the will to take the civil service examinations. Abandoning hope for rising through the system, such men who had "given up advancement" remained satisfied for life with the status of a *sheng-yüan.*

The examinations given as part of the examination system proper, as distinguished from the preliminary tests, were designed solely to select men for the bureaucracy and had nothing to do with education. After the Sung dynasty there were three main examinations: the provincial (*hsiang-shih*), the metropolitan (*hui-shih*), and finally the palace examination (*tien-shih*), this last conducted by the emperor himself. In time, however, another examination was added to check the scholarship of prospective candidates for the provincial examination and to limit the number of those actually admitted to the latter. On his first tour of the province a director of studies supervised the annual examinations, and on his second and last tour he conducted these special preliminary examinations. Indifferent to the former, licentiates took the latter examination very seriously, realizing that missing it would affect their careers, and they strove hard to win first place in it.

The results of these examinations, like those of the annual examinations, classified candidates into six grades. The best students in the first two grades automatically were permitted to take the provincial examination, although, to be sure, this dispensation was granted for one time only. The top five or ten candidates in the next grade also were admitted, but those below them were disqualified. Just before the provincial examination, however, the director of studies could assemble those disqualified students once again for another examination to fill any last-minute vacancies. The number of candidates passed at this time was about equal to that passed in the special preliminary examination.

The preliminary examination consisted of four parts: a question based on the Four Books; an essay on a political topic of the kind that would appear on all future examinations; a section on poetry; and, for the last time, a section of the Imperial Rescript. Since this last was composed for the instruction of beginners and commoners, the emperor himself held that there was no need to include it in higher examinations.

The number of candidates qualified to take the provincial examination (*chü-tzu*) was fixed at fifty-four to eighty-eight times the quota to be passed. But if extra space was available in the examination hall, more candidates would be admitted as a "bounty." In the end, it became usual for about a hundred candidates to compete for each position in the alloted quota.

CHAPTER FIVE

THE PROVINCIAL EXAMINATION
AND REEXAMINATION

THE DATE OF THE EXAMINATION   By law the provincial examination was given once every three years, that is, in the years of the rat, hare, horse, and cock. The specific time, too, was designated in advance: the first session was set for the ninth day of the eighth month in the Chinese calendar, followed by the second session on the twelfth day and the third on the fifteenth of the same month, with the proceedings ending on the sixteenth day. According to our modern calendar, this important examination took place in September, just a week before the harvest moon. Conscious of the hardships experienced by candidates, the government chose the time of year with the best weather.

When there was an important occasion in the palace, such as the enthronement of an emperor or a celebration of his long life or of the empress's, an extraordinary examination was authorized. Called an "examination by special grace," this reflected a change in the concept of the examinations: now they were regarded as acts of imperial generosity, opening the path for scholars eager to become officials, whereas originally they had been held by the emperor in order to recruit officials to assist him. When only one such extraordinary examination occurred between regular examinations there was no problem about timing; but if two special examinations came in the same year, it was the rule to advance one by half a year and to postpone the other for an equal interval.

THE DISPATCH OF EXAMINATION OFFICIALS   This examination was held in the provincial capital for all qualified candidates of the province. Officials for this temporary duty were selected and sent out by the central government, with one chief examiner (*cheng k'ao-kuan*) and one deputy examiner (*fu k'ao-kuan*) for each province. Officials eligible for such important assignments were convened at court in advance and commissioned after an examination. In order to forestall dishonesty, the place in which each examiner would serve was not decided until the last minute.

Arranging for the officials to reach their destinations punctually, the government timed the distances they must travel and dispatched them accordingly. For example, about ninety days were needed to go from Peking to Yünnan or Kweichow, the most distant provinces. Therefore, late in the fourth month high government officials proposed the names of the prospective examiners to the emperor, who then decided who should be the chief examiner and who the deputy. They were formally commissioned around the first day of the fifth month and had to set out for their goal within five days at the latest. After spending about three months on the journey, they would reach the capital of Yünnan or Kweichow a short time before the examination date, the ninth day of the eight month. For traveling to Kwangtung, Kwangsi, and Fukien, eighty days were estimated. For provinces closer to Peking, the length of time progressively decreased; thus, for Shantung, Shansi, and Honan the figure was twenty days. Journeys took that long because in those days travel was slow and inconvenient. Whenever possible, officials used such waterways as the Grand Canal and the Yangtze River. Since examination officials were imperial commissioners serving as the emperor's deputies, all other vessels yielded the right of way when a boat approached flying a banner bearing the characters *ch'in ch'ai,* "By Imperial Commission." Local officials, too, treated examiners with unfailing courtesy.

When they arrived in the provincial capital the examiners were welcomed by the governor general, the governor, the treasurer, the provincial judge, the prefect, and lesser officials, and they were introduced to the local officials who had been selected to assist in the examinations.

There were two types of assisting officials, examiners and administrators. Since the two officials sent by the central government could not attend to everything, local officials of outstanding scholarship were appointed by the governor general to serve as associate examiners (*t'ung k'ao-kuan*). In a large province there were eighteen such associates, while a small one had eight. Often prefects and magistrates (but never a schoolteacher) served in this capacity. These examiners were known also as "inner-section officials" (*nei-lien kuan*), to distinguish them from the "outer-section officials" (*wai-lien kuan*). These latter functionaries handled the essential administrative duties involved in the examination and were directed by a supervisor (*chien-lin kuan*), a post filled by the governor general or governor. Also on this supervisor's staff were men with specialized duties, such as answer collectors, regulators, inspectors, copyists, and proofreaders, who were not allowed to infringe upon each other's responsibilities.

THE EXAMINATION COMPOUND   In each provincial caiptal, there was
a permanent examination compound. Like a honeycomb, it was an
aggregation of thousands of single cells, each large enough to hold just
one man. Cell adjoined cell to form a barnlike tenement, the whole
maze occupying an extensive area.

In the southern capital, Chiang-ning-fu, for example, the Southern
Capital Examination Compound occupied a site north of the Ch'in-
huai Canal, famous for its pleasure boats. Three stone gates faced the
canal, and visible through them was the Great Gate, the entrance to
the examination compound. Within the Great Gate there was a large
open area with a second gate on the north. Beyond that stretched a
broad avenue (*yung-tao*), lined on both sides by the entrances to lanes
(*hao-t'ung*). Each lane was about two meters wide and disproportionately deep, extending farther than the eye could see. Lining one
side of each lane were countless small rooms or, more accurately,
cells. These examination cells (called *hao-she*, and also *hao-fang*) had
neither doors nor furniture and amounted to no more than spaces
partitioned on three sides by brick walls and covered by a roof. The
floors, naturally, were packed dirt. Each cell was equipped with only
three long boards. When placed across the cell from wall to wall, the
highest became a shelf, the middle one functioned as a desk, and the
lowest served as a seat. There were no other facilities: it was really
like a prison without bars. Here candidates taking the provincial
examination had to spend three days and two nights in succession.

The lanes were extraordinarily long: seemingly, one could walk
and walk without reaching an end. Because the building was used
only once in three years, usually it was in poor condition even if
occasional repairs were made. Shepherd's purse grew on the roof, the
eaves were on the verge of collapse, moisture stained the walls. Since
the lanes opened only at one end, a person walking in the wrong
direction would feel as though he were in a labyrinth; and if someone all by himself lost his way in such an eerie place at night, he
would have a weird, uncanny feeling, as though he heard the wailing
of a ghost. But if he walked in the right direction, he would emerge
on the broad avenue that led to the Great Gate.

Midway along that central avenue rose a splendid high building,
the Ming-yüan Lou, where a guard was maintained and signals were
sent during the examinations. There were also many tall watchtowers
(*liao-lou*), from which the candidates were observed in their doorless
cells. The activities of the candidates are said to have been well
under control. Actually, however, the place seems to have been too
huge to permit effective supervision, and the towers must have served
mainly as psychological deterrents.

North of the Ming-yüan Lou, on the grand avenue, were the quarters and offices of the examination staff, still more securely sur-rounded by a wall, with only one large gate. A great canal di-vided this area into a front part, for the administrative outer-section officials, and a back part, where the examiners were located. In accord with their duties, the outer-section officials had access to the examination site; but the inner-section officials, charged with judging the papers, were completely shut off in their quarters and could not leave the area until the grading was completed. They, too, were kept under strict physical restriction. A storehouse within the compound was filled with food ahead of time to sustain the hundreds of officials confined there for as long as a month.

Subdivided within and isolated by a great wall from the outside world, the whole examination compound had only one entrance, the Great Gate, which was used by the staff and the candidates alike. There was not a single small back gate. Only for receiving water and disposing of human waste were special arrangements made. A large quantity of water was required for the candidates' inkstones as well as for cooking and drinking. To meet this need there was a "water platform" (*shui-t'ai*) at the left and at the right of the Great Gate, where pure water was brought in from the outside. Before the ex-amination, laborers drew water from there and filled large jars placed at the entrance to each lane. These they replenished as needed. After that it was the candidate's chore to fetch the water he needed in an earthenware pot. After the examination, the human waste deposited in the toilet tubs placed at the end of each lane was collected by laborers and was bailed out from the cesspits of the waste-disposal facility at the eastern edge of the compound. Another such facility at the northern end of the compound served only the examination staff.

Otherwise the high outside wall did not have an opening large enough for an ant to get through. Thus, if a candidate died in the middle of an examination, the officials were presented with an an-noying problem. The latch bar on the Great Gate was tightly closed and sealed, and since it was absolutely never opened ahead of sched-ule, beleaguered administrators had no alternative but to wrap the body in straw matting and throw it over the wall.

AN ALL-NIGHT SESSION Minor administrative officials entered the compound on the fifth day of the eighth month and were searched to make certain that they did not bring in anything except essential clothing and personal effects. On the sixth day, after attending a small banquet given by the governor general and governor, the chief and deputy examiners entered the compound, accompanied by the supervisor (either the governor general or the governor), proctors (*t'i-tiao*) in charge of administration, and associate examiners. On the way to the compound the chief examiner and supervisor paraded through the city with the windows of their palanquins opened so that they could be seen by people in the streets. Their arrival at the compound was heralded by three cannon bursts fired from the Ming-yüan Lou, and then the heavy doors of the Great Gate were opened on the left and on the right to receive them. The other officials remained invisible inside while the supervisor, attended by his subordinates, inspected the compound thoroughly, determining whether the preparations had been carried out meticulously. Having once entered, all officials had to remain in the compound until the examination ended.

Meanwhile, candidates from throughout the province were steadily arriving in the capital. It is said that when they traveled by boat they hoisted a banner bearing the words "Applicant for the Imperially Decreed Provincial Examination of X Province," and passed through local customs stations without having their baggage checked. Once in the capital they went to the government reception station and bought folders of thick white answer sheets, which came in fourteen- and sixteen-page sizes. In both kinds of folders twenty-two lines, each with space for twenty-five characters, were printed in red on each page. In addition to three sets of answer sheets, a candidate needed paper for writing rough drafts. On the covers of the folders were spaces for entering the candidate's name, age, and distinctive physical characteristics. After filling in these spaces, each man turned over his folder to the authorities, receiving from them a receipt. On the day of the examination his folders would be returned to him in the compound.

On the eighth, the day before the beginning of the examination, the candidates entered the compound. Around midnight the first signal sounded, a single burst of cannon fire. Thirty minutes later two bursts were fired, and after thirty more minutes, three rounds announced the opening of the Great Gate, where the candidates gathered for the first roll call. They were divided according to their home districts into groups of from ten to a hundred men. These groups were identified by lanterns and banners. The candidates belonging to the first group assembled by a single lantern, on which "group one" was written. For the second group, two lanterns were hung side by side. When there were ten or more groups, five lanterns were hung in series, like those suspended from the roof of a festival float. Thus, the candidates could find their assembly points, even if they could not make out the characters in the dark. After dawn, they gathered under the appropriate banners.

During the roll call, instructors from each school verified the identity of each candidate. After the roll call, the groups passed through the Great Gate, one by one, each guided by a minor official. Personal attendants were not permitted beyond the Great Gate. As was to be expected, each candidate carried a large load, since he had to spend three days and two nights in the compound. He needed not only writing materials, such as an inkstone, ink, brushes, and a water pitcher, but also an earthenware pot, foodstuffs, bedding, and a curtain to hang across the entrance to his cell.

As soon as the candidates, carrying their heavy loads, had entered ihe compound through the Great Gate they were searched. Four soldiers at a time frisked one candidate from top to bottom and made him open his luggage for inspection. It goes without saying that books were forbidden, and so was any piece of paper with writing on it. Since a soldier who discovered such a paper was awarded three ounces of silver, the inspection was most stringent. It is said that the soldiers went so far as to cut open dumplings in order to examine their bean-jam fillings. Still, it was not rare to slip something past the strict eyes of the inspectors; during the worst times, some people maintained, enough books were brought in to stock a bookstore.

After this inspection, entry certificates were issued, but another search of personal belongings was made at the second gate; if any irregularity was discovered there, the first inspector, as well as the candidate himself, would be punished. After that the candidates came to the Dragon Gate, in front of which lay the grand avenue, flanked on each side by the openings of the lanes to the cells. Each lane was identified by a large character, taken in serial order from the *Primer of One Thousand Characters*. After finding and entering his lane, each candidate located his own cell, identified by a number. Then he put up the three boards and arranged his things. Since at least ten thousand men—at times as many as twenty thousand—entered the compound and had to be searched, the procedure used up most of a day. Those who got in during the early morning took a short, disturbed nap on their seats.

Generally one soldier was assigned as an attendant (*hao-chün*) for every twenty candidates. These soldiers, who were the lowest of the low in China's society, had only this opportunity to vent their resentment. Knowing that candidates who passed would follow the example of all officials and despise them as trash, these attendants shouted in loud voices to startle the candidates.

When the day-long commotion of entering the compound came to an end, and all the candidates were settled in their cells, the superintendent latched the Great Gate and sealed it. Now the candidates had to pass the night all alone in their cells, with nothing to do. Despite the good weather of midautumn, the cold air of a night wind easily penetrated the curtains of the open cells, and the thin bedding on the hard seat did not entirely keep out the cold. Worst of all, the cells were so narrow that the candidates could not stretch their legs to the full, but dozed off while bent over like shrimp. Their dreams, too, were certainly not tranquil. Especially those who had journeyed a long way from home probably saw, flickering before their eyes, the anxious faces of the parents, brothers, and friends they had left behind in their native villages.

Yet a still more compelling reason why they could not have enjoyed a good long sleep that night was the fact that the examination began early in the morning of the next day, while it was still dark. Accompanied by the loud shouts of the attendants, minor officials made the rounds and distributed the answer papers in exchange for the candidates' receipts. After they verified the name, age, and special physical traits noted on the cover, they stamped "checks" (*tui*) on the paper. Papers without this stamp were refused when the time came to hand in the answers.

The problems for this first day concerned three themes from the Four Books and the composition of a poem to a designated rhyme. The questions were printed on a disproportionately large piece of paper. On this question sheet several seals had been stamped, to indicate that all responsible officials had inspected and verified it. A copy of these questions was distributed to each candidate.

After receiving the questions the candidates placed their heads between their hands and racked their brains, setting about to draw up their answers. Plenty of time was given: they had until the evening of the following day, the tenth, to finish. After polishing their drafts on rough paper, they wrote out a clean copy when finally they had become sufficiently confident in their answers. While they suffered from anxiety, impatience, and various kinds of agitation in turn, time passed mercilessly. If they became hungry they ate the dumplings they had brought along, and those who had time to spare cooked rice in their earthenware pots. If rain fell during those two days, more than likely raindrops were blown by the wind into the doorless cells, and then the candidates desperately tried to shield their answer papers, more precious than life itself, making pathetic efforts to protect them although they themselves got wet. At night they were permitted to light a candle, but if it fell and burned a hole in the answer paper they were in trouble. Boys from good families, brought up carefully and never exposed even to a rough wind, had to fend for themselves, and for the only time in their pampered lives had to take care of everything by themselves alone. They were like raw recruits in an army.

When a candidate became tired at night, he could lay out his

bedding again and take a rest. But a bright light in a neighboring
cell would make him feel that he, too, should be hard at work, and so
he would get up again to face his paper. Suffering from fatigue, and
under heavy pressure, most candidates became a little strange in the
head, and many were unable to work at their best. In the most severe
cases, men became sick or insane.

HAUNTINGS BY GHOSTS A man who became ill or suffered an unexpected mishap in the examination compound fell into extreme dis-
grace, as though he had been caught in an immoral act, for—according to the concepts of religious Taoism widely accepted on all levels
of Chinese society—someone who secretly performed a good deed,
even if no one else knew about it, would one day receive good fortune, and he who committed an evil deed would be sure to suffer for
it. The most suitable place for such retribution, of course, was the examination compound.

The most dangerous vice for a scholar was "licentiousness," by
which was meant not a craze for dancing girls and the like, but the
ruination of a respectable woman. Candidates guilty of this offense
would fail at the crucial moment, no matter how bright they usually
were. There is, for instance, the story of a candidate who suddenly
went mad in the compound and began yelling, "Forgive me! Forgive
me!" On his answer sheet not a single character had been brushed,
only the picture of a girl's shoes, because he had been tormented and
driven insane by the ghost of a young maid who had committed suicide after he had seduced her. There are many similar tales, and it is
remarkable that those ghosts appeared mostly during the provincial
examinations. Perhaps this was because the candidates were confined
in the unnatural setting of the examination compound, away from
the authority and police power of local officials. People believed that
here alone was a place permitting revenge and that it was haunted by
spirits determined to be avenged.

Many such stories appear in the late Ch'ing collection *Ch'üan-chieh
Lu Hsüan*. One tells of a candidate who went to Nanking for the provincial examination and, wishing to stay overnight in an inn, bar-
gained with the proprietor over the charge. He said he was alone,
but the innkeeper disputed this: "Now, then, is your wife not right
behind you?" But when the candidate turned around, no one was
there. Then the innkeeper asked, "Is that pale lady not your wife?"
and the candidate suddenly turned pine-green, became all confused,
and, ending the conversation with the words, "The portents for this
examination are really bad—it is time to stop," fled at top speed.
With that the lady flared up at the innkeeper. "What kind of heartless man are you? Just as I discovered my enemy and sought to give

vent to my resentment, did he not escape solely on account of your gratuitous remarks?" Troubled, the innkeeper replied, "Since he left just a moment ago, how about quickly running after him? I know nothing about this."

"You know nothing about this! The point is that the examination compound is the only place in which the dead can obtain revenge. Just now I found my chance, but thanks to you it has been ruined. You wretch! What shall I do about you? After you have done this to me, I will take you back as a traveling companion instead. Give yourself up!" With these words she threw herself on the alarmed innkeeper, who answered, "Just a moment, please! I meant no harm. Mercy! There will be another chance, so please just wait for it. No matter how much it costs, I will pay your traveling expenses for your return to the land of the dead." Upon hearing this the lady recovered some of her good humor. After stipulating that the same evening he should burn paper money and offer a sutra for her, the bargain was completed and, with a grin, she vanished.

Again there is the story of the experience that befell Huang Yüeh, who obtained his *chin-shih* during the Ch'ien-lung era (1736–96) and rose to become director of the Board of Rites (*li-pu shang-shu*), equivalent to a minister of education. He went into the compound to take the examination and was sitting in his cell when a girl came flitting down his lane. Her dress was extremely shabby and her hair disheveled, but her face and figure were extraordinarily beautiful. Thinking this strange, because women were not allowed in the compound, he decided that she must surely be a ghost and called out to stop her. When he yelled, "Hey there, what does that spirit intend here?" the girl turned her head and answered, "Is it the great minister? It is not you, sir, I am visiting. Please excuse me this time." When she addressed him as "great minister" Huang Yüeh was elated, since ghosts had a supernatural power to see perfectly into the future. Drawing further courage from this, he settled down and calmly began questioning her. "In that case, who are you seeing?"

"Actually, Mr. X."

"He is a friend from my native village. Truly, what is your business here?"

"I must confess my shame so that you can understand why I am here. Please listen. I was the daughter of a tenant farmer who leased land from X. By chance he fell in love with me on first sight and begged me to marry him and become his secondary wife. At first I didn't take him seriously, but since he was so very earnest I was at last overcome by his affection, became his lover, and one day became pregnant. When this happened, his attitude suddenly changed. He became so heartless toward me that he broke his firm promise and in the end chose someone else for his secondary wife. My father, too, was anxious and went several times to negotiate with X. However, he not only would have nothing at all to do with my father but blamed me. Then I went myself, but the doorkeeper didn't let me pass. With no place to turn, I committed suicide by hanging myself. I bitterly hate that brute and am therefore about to kill him. Please let me go without interfering."

"Indeed, everything you told me sounds reasonable. Just listening to you makes me angry. Yet, to tell the truth, he is my best friend. So let us come to an understanding: would you consider some way to forgive him? Whatever you demand I will promise you on his behalf. First, he shall establish you as his principal wife. There shall be a formal marriage, and the engagement gift money shall be submitted to your father in full. If his present secondary wife should bear him a son, he shall be considered your son. If he himself or his son becomes eminent, you too shall be able to receive court rank. Would you consider changing your mind, from now on praying for his success, and also saving my face?"

As he desperately tried to persuade her with these words, the girl hid her face for a moment, but then agreed. "Perhaps this too is fated. I will entrust everything to you, sir." Huang then called X, who was nearby, to come. When X saw the girl, he changed color, fell on his knees before Huang, and tried to hide his head. While Huang cross-examined X, he only kept repeating, "Mercy, mercy!" When Huang explained the conditions of the agreement he had made with the girl, X, trembling and with teeth chattering, replied, "Yes, yes," and the girl recovered her good humor. "Well, in that case, all right. If I had not met you, sir, there is no telling where this would have ended, but thanks to you I too may attain buddhahood." With these words she disappeared. Huang and X both passed the examination brilliantly, succeeded in the subsequent examinations as well, obtained their *chin-shih* together, and finally became high ministers, while the girl was granted posthumous rank.

This story was said to have been told by a man who himself heard it from Minister Huang in his old age, but perhaps Huang merely used a ghost story to warn his friend when they entered the examination compound and get him to repent. This kind of situation was likely to occur among rich candidates, but such misconduct was dangerous for any candidate. To settle the ghost's grievance through arbitration is a typically Chinese solution, but the story also shows that there was something extraordinary about the atmosphere of the examination compound.

Many stories did not have a happy ending: often the man failed the examination or was haunted to death by a spirit. Thus, while a candidate was working over the organization of his answer during the second night of the examination, a cold wind suddenly blew into his cell and several times his candle seemed about to go out, when suddenly there appeared the pale face of a young nun. As, shocked, he was about to call out, the nun said, "Oh, this is not the place. Excuse me, I made a mistake," and disappeared. Just then the man in the next cell moaned aloud. There was the sound of a cross-examination, followed by insults, sobbing, and apologies, but suddenly the sounds stopped and it became perfectly still. When the man went to look in on his neighbor, he was dead.

When an answer paper was stained or a candidate was impelled by a strange urge to scribble something in a public place, he was penalized by being suspended from a number of subsequent examinations, thus reflecting the view that retribution for evil was carried out in the examination compound. After a certain candidate had stained his paper in this manner, he left the compound crestfallen, passed by the Ming-yüan Lou, and, as a warning to his juniors, recorded his thoughts upon the wall:

> From a thousand *li* I came to visit the capital,
> But, unknown to me, lamp oil stained my paper.
> It could only be because I have seduced three women.
> On the seventh try, who to blame for five suspensions?
> Now I realize: the powdered face was a goblin.
> I repent recklessly tying the marriage knot.
> Listen carefully, scholars with ambition:
> Beware of the beauty and fragrance of quietly blooming
>   flowers!

This poem probably concerns a love affair with a certain widow.

REWARDS FOR GOOD DEEDS   Just as evil deeds were punished in the examination compound, so also were good deeds rewarded there. For example, there is the story of a graduate from Soochow who always showed deep respect and concern for old people. When he entered the compound for the provincial examination, he immediately noticed an old man groaning in the cell next to his. Out of pity he exerted himself in different ways on behalf of this old man. When the latter groaned, probably suffering from a serious illness, the candidate took care of him by brewing some ginseng, which fortunately he had brought along, and giving it to him to drink. Having thus used up the time needed for writing his answer, he was in a great rush, when the old man told him, "I have already completed a rough copy of my answer. I think that for me it is an excellent composition, but I do not have the strength to write out a clean copy and would like to give it to you if it will help. Before I die, I want to see a paper written by myself pass with an excellent grade, even if it is not in my name.''

The young man found that it was really a fine piece of work and, pressed for time, hurriedly copied it and handed it in. And, lo and behold, it came in first. The Soochow region was the most culturally advanced in China, and since the area was known for its scholars, competition there was especially intense. Always, before the results of an examination were known, rumors circulated widely about who would win top place, but this time everyone was caught by surprise when a complete unknown ranked first.

When a candidate who had accumulated good deeds unknown to other ordinary men entered the compound, he would become clear-headed, like a changed man, and his answers would flow smoothly, as though spirits were lending a hand. It is said that when his answer reached the examiners, even if they tried to fail him, they were put into a state of mind in which they had to give him a high pass.

END OF THE EXAMINATION   At about six o'clock on the morning of the tenth day of the eighth month, the sound of cannon followed by some music signaled the end of the examination and indicated that it was time to hand in the answers. However, those who had not yet finished could remain behind and continue working until that evening. In this respect the system was relaxed and even generous.

Those who had finished writing handed in their papers at receiving counters arranged by district. Then the papers were thoroughly checked for violations of the formal regulations. Cutting out mis-written characters and pasting in a piece of paper, leaving blank spaces, skipping parts of a page, or handing in a completely white paper with no writing on it whatsoever were considered to be infractions of the rules. The name of anyone guilty of this kind of offense was posted outside the compound, and he was barred from taking future examinations. Those candidates whose papers were accepted received exit passes, packed their belongings, and left the compound through the Great Gate in large groups. That night they returned to their lodgings after an absence of two days, but they could not sleep there in comfort, for they had to get up in the middle of the night to enter the compound for the second time.

Early in the morning of the eleventh day, while it was still dark, again they gathered in front of the Great Gate, went through the roll call, and entered the compound shouldering their baggage. The next morning the second round of problems was distributed, this time five questions on the Five Classics. After writing out clean copies of their answers, the candidates had to reproduce several sentences from the opening paragraph of their answer to questions on the Four

Books written during the first session, or else add to the poem they had composed in the earlier test, in order to prove that the papers for the two examinations had been written by the same man. Forbidden to bring in or carry out any slips of paper, they had to rely on memory. For this reason, generally a discrepancy of up to ten characters was overlooked, but in case of a great discrepancy the man was presumed guilty of having used a substitute and was barred from examinations in the future.

The second session ended on the evening of the thirteenth day, and early the next morning the candidates entered the compound for the third session, which began in the very early morning of the fifteenth. This time there was an essay involving a broad critique of certain past or present government policies. It made little difference who selected the passages from the classics for the other tests, but this third session offered the chief examiner, who had been sent out from the capital far away and honored with an imperial edict, a valuable opportunity to show off his scholarship. Naturally he racked his brains to think up an appropriate question. It would be awkward if the question was too difficult and no one could answer it. To avoid this, the chief examiner sometimes prepared a lengthy question that in itself suggested the answer. At times this concern was carried so far that there were jokes about questions that became their own answers simply by removing the interrogative particle, the Chinese equivalent of our question mark.

Sometimes also there were strange orders from the court, to the effect that the essay question could not run over three hundred characters and the answer must not fall short of the same length. The questions were supposed to concern problems of statecraft from antiquity to the present, but since the Ch'ing was a foreign dynasty from Manchuria, much concerned with warning the Chinese against the notion of expelling foreigners, the examiners feared a slip of the brush and never set topics involving opinions on contemporary affairs. It was normal for the candidates, too, to write answers that were as inoffensive as possible.

The candidates were allowed until the evening of the following day, the sixteenth, to complete their papers; but since the essay did not require that much care, and the fifteenth was the day of the harvest moon, they usually wrote their essays, handed them in, and left the compound during that day. Then with the week-long examination over at last, they loosened the stiffness in their shoulders and feted the moon to their hearts' content.

THE COMPLEX GRADING SYSTEM   Having handed in their papers at last the candidates could relax, but now the onerous duties began for the examination staff. In the previous examinations, papers were graded and some men eliminated after each session, but in the provincial examination the papers from all three sessions had to be judged together. Since between ten and twenty thousand papers were submitted at each session they formed a mountainous pile that could be demolished only through a difficult and complex process.

Since the candidates' answers were written in black ink and absolutely no other color was permitted, they were called the "black versions" (*mo-chüan*). To guard against the possibility that the graders might show partiality to certain candidates whose writing they recognized, they were not shown the original papers. Instead, the black versions were copied by clerks in the outer section of the compound. Before that, however, the candidate's name, age, and other information about himself on the cover of the black version were concealed so that only the seat number remained visible. Then the black version was sent to the clerks to be copied on separate sheets of paper, this time using only vermilion ink, so that the copyists could not revise the original papers on their own initiative. Copying so many papers was hard work and required the services of several thousand clerks.

Next the vermilion copies (*chu-chüan*), together with the black originals, were passed on to the proofreaders, of whom there were several hundred. They made their corrections in yellow ink. Both copyists and proofreaders noted their names on the papers, to make clear their responsibility; needless to say, if any wrongdoing was discovered, those responsible were punished.

When the proofreading was completed, both versions were sent to the custodian, who retained the original and delivered the copy to the examiners in the inner section. The transfer of the copies through the single narrow door that connected the two sections took place under strict supervision.

The vermilion papers first passed through the hands of the associate examiners, who had to do the grading in designated places and were forbidden to carry a paper somewhere else on their own initiative. They used blue ink for their remarks and, by carefully reading the vermilion copies, decided in general upon passes and failures. When they wrote "mediocre" (*p'ing-t'o*) on the cover, or "without merit" (*shao ching-i*), or other such critical comments, the paper failed. When the paper was considered to be "excellent in style and content" (*pi-i ching-han*), they wrote "recommended" on the cover and then the paper was delivered to the chief and deputy examiners, who usually read only these recommended papers, although they were free to have other answer sheets brought to them.

It is said, however, that ordinarily they did not raise such an unrecommended paper above the fifteenth place, out of consideration for the face of the associate examiners. The chief and deputy examiners used black ink exclusively.

RECOMPENSE The candidate's ordeal was uncommonly hard, but the examiners, too, had to go through a great deal, occupied as they were day after day in demolishing that mountain of similar answers written in red ink. It is no wonder that they, too, sometimes became a bit strange in the head, and there are many tales of candidates who would have been doomed without the assistance of a watchful spirit during the time of grading.

A certain examiner read an answer that was completely without merit and, intending to fail it, took up his brush, when from somewhere he heard a voice say, "No!" He then tried rereading the paper but still could not find anything good in it at all. When he tried again to take up his brush and fail it, there was a cry: "No! No!" He found this really strange and wondered if he himself was suffering from nerves, but, deciding that there was no reason to think so, he picked up his brush for the third time and again clearly heard the voice say, "No! No!" Thinking that special circumstances must be involved, he reconsidered, and when he picked up his brush, this time to write a passing grade, nothing happened. After the announcement of the results he summoned the author of the paper, who turned out to have practiced medicine on the side. When the examiner recounted the incident and asked for an explanation, the candidate thought for a while, then slapped his knee and told the following tale:

"Once I examined a poor student who was ill and, out of sympathy, did not charge him a fee or ask him to pay my transportation costs. As a result, he was saved from death. Once when I was staying overnight in his house, his wife entered my room in the middle of the night and said, 'Although I want to pay the medical fee, I have nothing; so at least just this one night allow me to comfort you.' Taken aback, I answered, 'I will tell your mother-in-law what you have said,' but she replied, 'Actually, she ordered me to do this.' When I answered, 'In that case, I will tell your husband,' she answered, 'My husband's life was saved, thanks to you. It is with his consent, too.' Hearing this, since I, too, am not made of wood or stone, I was a bit tempted, but, aware that this could not be, pulled myself together and exclaimed, 'No, no.' However, the wife said, 'If I leave it at this and depart, I will be scolded by my mother-in-law,' and instead of leaving, she sat down. The night grew late and, on the point of succumbing to the temptation, I, aware that it could not be, strained every nerve, and while writing 'No! No!' on a paper upon the desk, continued to reproach myself, and finally held out until morning."

According to another story, a tired examiner, when beginning to read an answer, inadvertently rested his head upon the desk and, briefly dozing, had a dream in which an old woman appeared, who said, "The paper you are about to read is by my grandson. The King of the Dead, as a reward for the good life led by my grandson, gave me leave to look after his paper. Won't you please give him a good grade?" Uneasy about this, the examiner put the paper aside for a while but, not wishing to be influenced by such a dream, decided to fail the paper. But the old woman reappeared in a dream that night and earnestly appealed to him. "The father of this boy performed a unique good deed. He discovered that a prisoner condemned to death was innocent and got him acquitted. The fact that his son nevertheless appears to be failing reflects on the authority of the King of the Dead." The examiner, thinking that there might be something in this, had two of the candidate's papers brought and found them unusually well written. Therefore he finally decided to pass him in the whole examination. Later, after the results had been announced at last, he took out the answers again and found that there was nothing special about any of the grandson's papers.

In another case an associate examiner discovered an outstanding answer among the papers in his charge and forwarded it to the chief examiner with a recommendation that it be given first place. The chief examiner, too, read and admired it as a good piece of work, but in a dream that night the King of the Dead appeared to him and said, "That answer cannot be accepted. Look at this. It is like this," whereupon he opened his palm, on which was written *yin,* the character for "licentious." The next day, when the chief examiner again went to work on the papers, he completely forgot about the dream. But when he gathered the very best papers to make his final decision, he suddenly saw that in one place in this candidate's answer there was a violation of form. Before he forgot, he took up his brush and marked the place with an X. The associate examiner saw this and said, "This does not amount to a violation of form. And if it were a violation, there are many cases like it in these answers." Then he immediately showed the chief examiner other answers in the same form. The chief examiner regretted what he had done and sprinkled water on the X to wash it out. Ordinarily it could have been erased easily, but the more he washed it the clearer the X became, and at last he gave up and failed the paper. When later he made inquiries, he learned that the author excelled in scholarship but was notorious for his improper conduct.

In still another case an examiner thought an answer was really poor and marked it with an X. Then suddenly a strange breeze blew out his light. Because it was already late at night and he was tired, he went to bed. But when he got up next morning and looked at the paper, the X had disappeared. No matter how he held the paper to the light, there was no trace of it whatsoever. Surprised, he passed the paper in the lowest place, and, sure enough, it is said that its author was a splendid man who later became a famous statesman.

When the grading was completed, the results of the three examinations were averaged and the final decisions were reached about who should be passed. The number to be passed was fixed for each province, with more than ninety places allowed for a large province and forty for a small one. As a prize for effort, a list of runners-up (*fu-pang*) was made public, consisting of one man for every five who passed. These, too, received certain privileges.

Not knowing the names of the candidates, the examiners used the seat numbers in compiling their several lists. Then they met with the administrative officials of the outer section, and in their presence compared the vermilion copies with the originals. If these matched, the examiners broke the seal on the cover of the original answer papers to reveal the candidate's name. First the assistant examiner wrote the character *ch'ü* in black upon the red-ink copy, and then the chief examiner wrote *chung* beneath it, forming the compound *ch'ü-chung*, meaning "passed." Next the assistant examiner wrote the names of the candidates on the red-ink copies, one after another. The two sets of answers were carefully preserved, and in due course the black-ink originals were forwarded to the Board of Rites in Peking (which may be thought of as the central ministry of education), where they were examined once more.

For the announcement of the results, the examination staff brought out a large placard on which, in full public view, they wrote the names of the successful candidates in sequence. Using a piece of white paper bearing a drawing of a dragon on the right and a tiger on the left, they left blank a small space at the beginning and wrote out the names from the sixth man on down. After writing the last name, they rested for a while. The candidates whose names had appeared were very happy; the others, even though most of them would be failures, still clung to a thin thread of hope, since it was not impossible that they might be among the top five names yet to be announced. At last the members of the staff returned, and as they wrote in the first five names, the crowd applauded. When the supervisor finished his inspection and affixed his great seal to the list, everything was over. Generally this announcement took place between the fifth and the twenty-fifth day of the ninth month.

Those who hab passed were no longer students, but would hold their newly acquired status of "graduate," or *chü-jen,* for the rest of their lives. *Chü-jen,* literally "recommended man," here translated as "graduate," can also be translated as "master of arts," but conveys a much higher status than does any of these terms. Aside from being qualified to take the metropolitan examination in Peking during the third month of the following year, and every third year thereafter, a *chü-jen* could hold certain offices. The man who passed in first place (*chieh-yüan*) gained great prestige.

Among the new graduates, some returned home to rest. The governor general of the province sent to each prefecture the names of its successful candidates, and the prefect passed the news down to the district magistrate, who in turn informed the man himself. The notice was printed on a large sheet of red paper like that used for the qualifying examination, and it too was called a "victory announcement." After receiving the good news, the graduates reassembled in the provincial capital to thank the examiners for their grace.

The examination staff, for their part, released from their long confinement, were able at long last to lay down their heavy burdens. The delight of the specially dispatched chief and associate examiners at the termination of their duties can easily be imagined. They, together with the assistant examiners, invited the new graduates to a congratulatory feast known as the Banquet of Auspicious Omen or, more literally, Deer-cry Banquet (*lu-ming yen*). If any old men who had passed the provincial examination sixty years before were in the area, they also were invited to the occasion, which then was called the Second Banquet of Auspicious Omen in celebration of this grand event in the scholarly world. Moreover, if the son or grandson of such an old man was among the new graduates, he was "adding flowers to the brocade" and the event was made even happier because it meant not only that the young man had passed the provincial examination very early in life but also that the elder had attained considerable longevity.

All guests first turned in the direction of Peking to render their thanks for the imperial grace, and then the banquet began to the sound of music. The text for this music was the poem from the *Book of Poetry,* "*Yu, yu,* cry the deer," which describes a memorable entertainment given by an emperor for his officials and guests. Then the new graduates paid their respects to the examiners, whom they considered their lifelong teachers, and entered into a firm master-disciple pledge. The chief and associate examiners were called "master teacher" (*tso-shih*), and the assistant examiners "teacher" (*fang-*

shih), while the graduates called themselves "disciples" (*men-sheng*) and referred to each other as "classmates" (*t'ung-nien*).

In earlier times the master-disciple relationship had been formed between the teacher who personally taught and the student who actually received instruction, but after the examination system became dominant a change took place and only the examiners were honored as masters. The men who actually taught the students were simply called "teachers from whom we receive instruction" and were not given much credit. In what was a hard, clear-cut business transaction, the students considered their obligations to teachers fulfilled when they paid the exact tuition fee. In contrast, the graduate felt very grateful for being appreciated by the court-commissioned examiner, who, free to determine who was qualified, had selected him from among many competitors. The examiner read the answer only once, but the graduate remained grateful to him for the rest of his life. The result was a pledge between them to assist each other to weather the storms of official life. This practice was very undesirable from the imperial point of view, because it tended to further bureaucratic factionalism, but no matter how often prohibitions were issued against it they had not the slightest effect.

THE SEVEN TRANSFORMATIONS OF A CANDIDATE Those candidates who passed the provincial examination and became graduates rose in social status above the ordinary man, but before reaching these heights they were subjected to very harsh treatment. With some reason, critics charged that these were not examinations of scholarship but tests of brute physical strength. Others said that to pass the provincial examination a man needed the spiritual strength of a dragon-horse, the physique of a donkey, the insensitivity of a wood louse, and the endurance of a camel.

P'u Sung-ling (1640–1715) was a literary man who failed the provincial examination many times and never did become a graduate. He wrote a satire about the seven transformations of a candidate:

When he first enters the examination compound and walks along, panting under his heavy load of luggage, he is just like a beggar. Next, while undergoing the personal body search and being scolded by the clerks and shouted at by the soldiers, he is just like a prisoner. When he finally enters his cell and, along with the other candidates, stretches his neck to peer out, he is just like the larva of a bee. When the examination is finished at last and he leaves, his mind in a haze and his legs tottering, he is just like a sick bird that has been released from a cage. While he is wondering when the results will be announced and waiting to learn whether he passed or failed, so nervous that he is startled even by the rustling of the trees and the grass and is unable to sit or stand still, his restlessness is like that of a monkey on a leash. When at last the results are announced and he has definitely failed, he loses his vitality like one dead, rolls over on his side, and lies there without moving, like a poisoned fly. Then, when he pulls himself together and stands up, he is provoked by every sight and sound, gradually flings away everything within his reach, and complains of the illiteracy of the examiners. When he calms down at last, he finds everything in the room broken. At this time he is like a pigeon smashing its own precious eggs. These are the seven transformations of a candidate.

THE THIN LINE BETWEEN FAILURE AND SUCCESS It is extremely difficult to be absolutely fair in preparing or grading any examination, and even present-day "objective" tests do not succeed completely in this respect. The results were still more questionable in the Chinese examination system, where the long answers were read in a great hurry by examiners who often were not in a state of mind to judge them carefully. There was a saying that a candidate's showing in the examinations had nothing to do with his scholarship or writing skill but was entirely a matter of luck. Such a belief at least consoled those who failed.

Wu Ching-tzu (1701–54) was the author of the great satirical novel *Ju-lin Wai-shih* (*The Scholars*), in which he recorded what he had heard in the scholarly world. In a humorous vein he depicted the experience of one Fan Chin, who was taking the qualifying examination to become a *sheng-yüan*:

When Chou Chin, the Director of Education for Kwangtung, was conducting the qualifying examination in the provincial capital, he noticed a student with a yellowed face, hollow cheeks, and white hair sitting in his seat. Before long this student came to hand in his answer, and when the examiner looked at him closely, he saw that his clothes were tattered and that he appeared very needy. Chou Chin checked his name and saw that he had given his age as thirty. The following conversation ensued:

"Is your name Fan Chin?"

"Yes, sir, I am Fan Chin."

"How old are you?"

"It should be registered as thirty, but actually I am fifty-four."

"How many times have you taken the examination?"

"I first took it when I was twenty, and this is my twentieth time."

"Why have you been unable to pass for such a long time?"

"Somehow my compositions were so poor that I always failed."

"I doubt that. Please leave. I will definitely look at it."

When Fan Chin had left the hall Chou Chin waited a while, and since no one else came to hand in his paper, he picked up Fan Chin's answer and tried to skim through it, thinking in his heart, "This is miserable. It is, after all, impossible." Chou Chin waited a while, but when still no one else came to hand in his paper, he took up Fan Chin's answer once more and, fidgeting, reread it two or three times, hoping he would find some redeeming feature. Then gradually he became aware that it was a very sophisticated composition. In the end he involuntarily sighed. "This is a superb essay. After reading it only once or twice I could not understand its fine points, but on the third reading, I at last realized that it is one of the best pieces of prose in the world. What a shame that the hard-headed examination officials have brought to tears many truly brilliant intellects like this man!"

This took place in the qualifying examination, when only about half the candidates were failed. The attrition was still worse in the provincial examination, when at best one in a hundred candidates was passed, and the sheer number of papers made it most difficult to select, say, a hundred papers out of ten thousand. It is understandable that such a famous literary man as P'u Sung-ling was unsuccessful to the very end.

THE EMINENCE OF A GRADUATE   On becoming a graduate a man's status in the eyes of the world changed overnight. In *The Scholars* there is an account of what happened to the fictional Fan Chin when he passed the provincial examination:

Fan Chin had at last passed the qualifying examination and become a *sheng-yüan*, but he was still poor. Even when he went out there were always shreds hanging from the bottom of his robe, so he was not much respected by the world. Especially hard on Fan Chin was his wife's father, a stubborn old man known as Old Mister Hu of the butcher shop, or Butcher Hu. Since Fan Chin, oblivious to his wife's hardships, usually immersed himself in his studies, he was always abused and scolded by his father-in-law. When the date for the provincial examination approached, Fan Chin wanted to go to the provincial capital. Swallowing his pride, he went to Butcher Hu to borrow money for the journey, but far from advancing him the money, Butcher Hu heaped abuses on him and made Fan beat a hasty retreat. Fortunately he had a friend who lent him the money and in the end he went to the capital, took the examination, and returned home, only to find that his wife and mother, having run out of food, had already gone two or three days without rice and were on the verge of death by starvation. When he got wind of this Butcher Hu began to shout. And Fan Chin went to town carrying a one-winged chicken to sell for rice money.

While he was out three messengers came on horseback from the district office, bringing Fan Chin's "victory announcement," the notice that he had passed the provincial examination. After that a great many messengers, taking turns on the horse, came to offer their congratulations in the hope of getting a tip, and when not even a small tip was forthcoming they remained there. Furthermore, as soon as people in the neighborhood heard about this, they came crowding in to offer their congratulations, so that the doorway was blocked and there was great confusion, as at the scene of a fire.

When some bystanders saw Fan Chin plodding home crestfallen and still holding the chicken, too lean to attract a buyer, they called to him, "You passed, you passed!" but he did not take them in the least seriously. But when he got to his house he saw posted on his door a large crimson sheet, which read:

VICTORY NOTICE

May your name always appear as an outstanding pass in the Official Gazette!
The Honorable Fan Chin has passed the Kwangtung Provincial Examination in Seventh Place.

Seeing this, Fan Chin called out the single word, "Passed," and collapsed in a faint. When his mother, flustered, filled a bucket and dashed water on his head, he revived all right but went running around saying, "I've passed, I've passed!" He had gone completely out of his mind. Among the messengers from the district office there was a clever man, who now turned to the bystanders and told them, "The new graduate, carried away by joy, has lost his mind. It often happens at such times that, if a man is scolded by the one whom he normally fears most, he will be cured." Deciding that that was an excellent idea, they sent someone to fetch Butcher Hu. As always, Hu was selling meat in town, and when he heard the news he came, rubbing his eyes, half believing and half in disbelief. At last he raised his hand to give his son-in-law a blow on the head. Usually he would have proceeded without hesitation, but this time it was different, for now the man he was facing was a graduate. "No! Dear me! True, he is my son-in-law, but from now on he is a graduate. Is it not said that to become a graduate is to become a star in the heavens? If I should beat a star I would be carried off by the King of the Dead, and receive a hundred blows with a club, and end up sinking to the eighteenth subterranean hell, never to rise again for all eternity."

However, the bystanders, all together, talked him round: "Listen, big man, are you not by trade a butcher who, day after day, from morning until evening, stains your white kitchen knife red by killing pigs, slaughtering hogs, cutting the meat up into pieces, and selling it? You are already properly recorded in the register of the King of the Dead, and it has been decided that you will sink into hell when you die. However, if now you make a strenuous effort and cure your son-in-law's illness, the merit of the deed will raise you up to the seventeenth hell."

Finding this argument irresistible, Butcher Hu called for wine to give him courage, gulped down two bowls, and, emboldened by this slightly tipsy state, rolled up his sleeves and again seemed his old self about to handle a pig. Fan Chin's mother now became frightened and cried, "Please do not hit him too hard. I ask that you not wound him. It will be fine if you just give him a shock." Butcher Hu chased after Fan Chin, who was still running around, and seized him with all his might, while Fan kept shouting, "I've passed! I've passed!" Hu roared at Fan, "Swine, what's this about passing?" and struck him. But after landing one blow, he did not have the courage to raise his hand again. Fortunately, Fan Chin, knocked to the ground, momentarily lost consciousness, and when he revived was back to normal.

A CASE OF OFFICIAL MALFEASANCE   The original black-ink versions of the passing examination papers were checked against the red-ink copies and forwarded to the capital at Peking, where forty officials were assigned by the Board of Rites to examine yet again the answers collected from all over the country. They decided whether the papers were worth passing and also checked for violations of form. If they discovered an irregularity the author's dearly won status of graduate was canceled.

This higher inspection also involved checking up on the examiners who had corrected the papers, particularly if violations of form and similar mistakes had been allowed to slip through as a result of a reader's error. If a simple honest mistake had been made, the matter was allowed to rest; but if investigation disclosed that the examination official had taken a bribe and intentionally manipulated matters, it turned into a most serious affair. There were, to be sure, detailed laws to prevent malfeasance in the examinations, but after all, men were the ones who enforced those laws. In the late Ch'ing period administration was lax, and it was common talk that examiners took bribes from candidates. If an examiner plotted with a candidate there were any number of ways to get around the regulations. They could arrange, for instance, that the examiner should pass a paper in which a certain character appeared in a certain space on a certain line; thus, with an innocent air, the examiner would give his man a high grade even though he did not know his seat number. If he did know the seat number, that made his trickery all the easier.

After the provincial examination in 1858 there was a great scandal. Emperor Hsien-feng (r. 1851–62), by nature a nervous man, had been greatly disturbed by the Taiping Rebellion, which was intensifying in fury in the south, and by the joint English and French forces that in addition to occupying Kwangtung were advancing on Tientsin, when a case of official misconduct was discovered in one of the provincial examinations. During the inspection of the passing papers, an answer turned up that because of a violation of form under no circumstances should have been passed. Further careful investigation revealed that, out of fifty questionable papers, twenty had definitely been passed dishonestly. When the key man was called for interrogation it became clear that not only the associate examiner but high officials up to Chief Examiner Po Sui were implicated. An associate examiner named P'u An had been asked by an official to pass the candidate Lo Hung-i. Since an associate examiner was powerless by himself, P'u enlisted the cooperation of Chief Examiner Po Sui. Using a code word, they sought out Lo's paper, which had been failed by another associate examiner, and arranged to substitute it for one that had passed. At the same time, in a separate case, the son of another associate examiner, Ch'eng T'ing-kuei, eager to take advantage of the opportunity for making some easy money, took bribes here and there and sent his father letters containing the code words. The father, suffering pangs of conscience, did not pass the men depending upon him, but was guilty of breaking the regulation requiring him to denounce his son's activities.

Punishment was most severe. Chief Examiner Po Sui, Associate Examiner P'u An, Candidate Lo Hung-i, the official who had made the arrangements for Lo, and the son of Associate Examiner Ch'eng T'ing-kuei were sentenced to death. In the case of Ch'eng T'ing-kuei himself the death penalty was commuted and his punishment was lowered by one degree, to banishment to a distance of three thousand *li,* or about one thousand miles, from Peking. Although the assistant examiners were not involved in the plot, they were heavily punished for negligence in not uncovering the malfeasance of their colleagues. The graduates who had written the answers containing the violations of form were stripped of all previous academic credentials, and the examination administrators who had not noticed what was happening were penalized in the same way. Even the high official who had ordered the investigation after the case was uncovered was punished on the grounds that the procedure had been lax.

Inasmuch as Chief Examiner Po Sui, who had been condemned to death, was an official of the highest rank, this scandal caused a great sensation throughout the land, and for a while the examinations were conducted honestly. But it is a sad commentary upon the morality of bureaucrats that such harsh measures were necessary at all, and when the memory of this severe purge grew faint, abuses appeared again. By the end of the nineteenth century an atmosphere of hopeless decay permeated the examination compound. The examination system itself was abolished early in the twentieth century.

EXAMINATION LORE Passing examination papers were sent to Peking, but what was done with the great mass of papers that failed? These could be retrieved by their authors at the examination compound for a small handling charge. Thus the staff made some money, while the candidates are said to have profited considerably from reading the examiners' comments.

Papers that no one picked up were burned in a special "caring for writing" incinerator (*hsi-tzu lu*) set up in the examination compound, indicating the respect shown the written word. Often such paper-incinerators were placed outside the compound, at street corners and the like, since anyone at all concerned about scholarship must respect paper with writing upon it and should not step on such paper or scatter it about. It was said that a man who neglected a piece of paper bearing the revered characters was punished with repeated failure in examinations; while, in contrast, he who gathered such papers and burned them earned enough merit to achieve a pass.

Before the passing papers were sent to Peking, the red copies of the ten best sets of answers were collected into a separate package and forwarded to the capital for the emperor's personal inspection. Furthermore, on some occasions the top five answers were printed and distributed by the examination officials, who this time could not add their own comments. Even candidates whose papers were not really very good could print their answers and distribute those black-ink versions to relatives and friends. Bookstores, always looking for means to profit, were forbidden to print and sell them as model answers.

Because the provincial examination was difficult, white-haired *sheng-yüan* frequently came to take it. Therefore the government established special provisions for such old men. In the beginning, candidates seventy years of age or older were passed outside the quota, regardless of the quality of their answers, just as long as they had not violated any of the formal rules. Later, however, because there were too many of them, the age was raised to eighty and above. The reason for at first setting the limit at seventy years lay in the fact that, because this was the retirement age for officials, such ancient candidates could no longer hope for an official career. All they could do was obtain an honorary degree and boast about it to their children and grandchildren.

THE REEXAMINATION OF GRADUATES   In the third month of the year following the provincial examination, graduates from the entire country gathered in Peking for the metropolitan examination. Since that was held not only for new graduates but for everyone who had ever passed a provincial examination, the number of candidates came to well over ten thousand. In order to avoid the danger that more graduates might appear than would fit into the Peking Examination Compound, still another examination was instituted during the Ch'ing dynasty. This reexamination took place a month before the session in Peking, on the fifteenth day of the second month.

As credentials each graduate brought a letter of introduction from his governor general or governor addressed to the Board of Rites. When he left his native place he also received from his province some official travel-expense funds, *kung-ch'e-fei,* inasmuch as candidates going to the metropolitan examination, one of the loftiest of governmental functions, were considered to be engaged in a kind of official business. For the same reason carriages and boats bearing the candidates flew a banner saying "Participant in the Board of Rites Metropolitan Examination Held by Imperial Decree" (*feng-chih li-pu hui-shih*). When officials saw this banner they ceded the right of way. Those candidates who traveled by land from faraway places, such as Sinkiang, were especially provided with official post horses, escorted from post station to post station, and treated with all courtesy.

On the day before the reexamination the Board of Rites petitioned the emperor, requesting the appointment of examination officials, and the emperor commissioned several high ministers as examiners (*yüeh-chüan ta-ch'en*). As soon as those examiners received the sealed packet of questions from the emperor, they went to the examination compound. There they opened the packet, had the questions printed, and saw that everything else was in order for the following day.

The subject matter for the reexamination was one topic from the Four Books and one poem. The examination itself needed only one day; and the examiners were commanded to complete the grading within four days. The results were divided into five groups. When the list was ready it was sent to the emperor, who turned it over to a different set of examiners. They compared the answers with those the candidate had written on the provincial examination, checked to see whether the calligraphy was identical, reviewed the appropriateness of the first examiner's grades, and, if all was well, announced the results. Those candidates who had been ranked in the top three groups were permitted to take the next metropolitan examination without further difficulty, but the right of those in the fourth group to take the examination was suspended from one to three times, depending on how badly they had fared. Those listed in the fifth group were deprived of their status as graduates and reduced to the rank of commoner.

For those candidates who missed the announced date, there was a supplementary examination (*pu-fu*) on the twenty-fourth day of the second month. Men who were not able to take this examination, either, were unable to participate in the metropolitan examination for that year. To alleviate congestion, candidates from the vicinity of Peking were given the reexamination immediately following their provincial examination; those who missed that date took the supplementary examination, together with the candidates from the rest of the country who had missed the reexamination.

CHAPTER SIX

THE METROPOLITAN EXAMINATION
AND REEXAMINATION

THE METROPOLITAN EXAMINATION (*hui-shih*, also known as *kung-chü*) was given in the Peking Examination Compound to graduates who had qualified in the reexamination. It was held in the third month of the year, after the provincial examination, and thus came in the years of the ox, dragon, sheep, and dog. Historically, the metropolitan examination was the heart of the examination system, with the preceding provincial examination counting merely as a preparation and the subsequent palace examination serving simply as yet another reexamination. During the T'ang dynasty the *hui-shih* led directly to the *chin-shih* degree.

The metropolitan examination, like the provincial, consisted of three consecutive sessions. The first began on the ninth day of the third month, the second on the twelfth day, and the third on the fifteenth day. In charge was the minister of rites (*li-pu shang-shu*), who functioned as a minister of education and in this case was called *chih kung-chü*, the old T'ang title for metropolitan examination supervisor. One chief, three deputy, and eighteen associate examiners (*cheng k'ao-kuan, fu k'ao-kuan,* and *t'ung k'ao-kuan,* respectively, as in the provincial examination) were especially designated by the emperor. As soon as they received their commissions, on the sixth day of the third month, they entered the compound, to remain confined there until the end of the examination. When the chief examiner accepted his commission he was also given the key to a box, which he would receive later, containing the questions placed in it by the emperor. In principle the questions for the first round were set by the emperor himself; if in practice he followed the suggestions of high ministers, the final decision was still his.

On the morning of the eighth, the day before the first session, after forming themselves into groups of fifty from each province and undergoing inspection, the graduates began entering the compound. On the same day the minister of rites received the question box from the emperor, took it to the compound, and personally turned it over to the chief examiner, who immediately unlocked it so that he could have the questions printed in the compound. On the morning of the ninth the printed questions were distributed to the candidates. This time there were three questions on the Four Books and a poem to occupy the candidates, groaning away in their cubicles through the night. On the morning of the tenth they handed in their papers and left the compound.

They returned the next morning to be ready for the second round, which began on the twelfth. This time there were five questions upon the Five Classics, selected by the chief examiner, not by the emperor. This second session ended on the thirteenth. The candidates reentered the compound on the day before the next and final session, which called for five essays. Once again the chief examiner set the questions, submitting them to the emperor for his approval.

After the examiners graded the papers and decided on the overall standing of the candidates, listing them by seat number, the minister of rites in his capacity as supervisor of the examination petitioned the emperor for his approval. Red-ink copies of the ten best papers were presented to the emperor by the chief examiner, so that he himself could rank them and make the decision about the number of men to be passed. Originally there was no fixed quota; and once, during a shortage of officials early in the Ch'ing dynasty, it even happened that more than 400 candidates were approved. Then in the K'ang-hsi era (1662–1723) there was a surplus of men qualified for office, so the quota was reduced to about 150. Late in the K'ang-hsi era, however, in order to give men from distant areas a chance, provincial quotas were set, ranging from 20 men for a large province to just a few for a small one, with a grand total of about 200 each year for the entire country. Late in the dynasty the number was increased again, to 300 annually.

When the emperor had finished with the papers the minister of rites took the results to the examination compound, where, together with the examiners, he supervised the verification of the red-ink copies against the black-ink originals, made out the lists of names, and issued the results on a placard set up for all to see on a beautifully decorated platform (*ts'ai-t'ing*) previously erected in front of the Board of Rites. This event usually took place before the fifteenth day of the fourth month, and marked the release of the examination staff from their confinement in the compound.

Although the metropolitan examination was given in a provincial-examination compound, followed procedures identical with those of the provincial examination, and required candidates to spend three days and two nights in uncanny cells, the appearance of ghosts was surprisingly uncommon. Perhaps because their nerves had already been tempered by the provincial examination, few of the graduates facing the metropolitan examination were victims of nerves. But cases of retribution and strange apparitions were not totally unknown; and even a graduate could not afford to be careless, as the following case shows.

A certain graduate had two friends, one of whom was much taken with the beauty of the other's wife and would stop at nothing to bring about a divorce. He consulted the graduate and in the end got him, by a generous financial offer, to spread rumors concerning his friend's wife. Dejected, the hapless husband consulted, of all people, the graduate, who advised him to divorce her and on the spot wrote out a rough draft of a divorce letter, which he got the man to copy. Just then a brush-seller came by, and the graduate purchased a large brush to use in the next metropolitan examination. Not thinking about what he was doing, he rolled up the draft letter and stuffed it into the hollow stem of the brush. He had forgotten all about this when he took the brush into the Peking Examination Compound, where the draft was discovered during the prescribed inspection. The letter had nothing to do with the classics, but according to the regulations, anything with writing on it was strictly forbidden. The inspector, an illiterate soldier, immediately reported the matter to his superior, who, galled by the insolent draft, enforced the law without mercy. In addition to losing his status as a graduate, the man was beaten on the back and exposed for several days to public view in front of the gate. It was unusual to carry the inspection as far as the stem of a brush; gossips said that this time it was caused by the powerful curse of the divorced woman.

At another metropolitan examination an examiner discovered a superb paper and intended to recommend it for first place. That night the King of the Dead appeared to him in a dream and said, "Fail that paper. It is written by Graduate So-and-so from T'aichou, a village shyster, who has repeatedly done wrong by dragging people into lawsuits and even caused men to die for no crime at all." Thereupon the examiner changed his mind and decided to fail him. Later, when he checked the seat number against the name, the author's identity and native place were exactly as given by the King of the Dead. Soon the man himself died in his dormitory in Peking.

In another case, a forty-year-old *sheng-yüan* named Lin, discouraged at not yet having passed even the provincial examination, was thinking of abandoning the examinations as hopeless and entering business when he heard a voice from somewhere say, "Do not lose heart!" Looking around and not finding anyone, he thought it was some kind of spirit and called out, "Who are you who say so?" The answer came: "I am a ghost." When he said, "Appear if you are a ghost," the ghost warned, "I will gladly appear, but you will be shocked by the sight of me," and let itself be seen: a dreadful green face, dripping with blood. The ghost said, "I have one wish. I was a country cloth-dealer and was killed by a wicked fellow, who buried my corpse under a great stone mortar within the city walls. Now, you are an important man who in the future will become a magistrate of my district, and I, constantly anxious about your welfare, have come to protect you because I believe that, when you take up your duties in my prefecture in the near future, you will clear up the wrong done to me. By no means lose heart, for you will certainly pass in the next provincial examination, definitely succeed in the subsequent metropolitan examination, and become a *chin-shih.*" Then the apparition vanished.

Lin recovered his courage, entered the next provincial examination, really did pass it, and became a graduate. But he failed the next metropolitan examination. On his way back to his lodgings on the day the results were announced, he muttered to himself, "The ghost is not entirely reliable after all." But immediately the same voice as before said, "That is your fault. I was not mistaken. Please reflect well on what happened on such-and-such a day. If you repent, you will be let off with merely a three-year delay." Thinking about it, Lin remembered how on that day he had set about seducing a certain widow. Realizing this, he carefully behaved himself from then on and suppressed all sexual desire. As a result, he passed the next examination, also got through the palace examination without any trouble, became a *chin-shih,* and was assigned as a magistrate to the dead man's district. When, on his inspection of the city, Magistrate Lin approached the east gate, he saw a large stone mortar, just as the ghost had predicted. Upon moving it, a decayed corpse was found. Lin immediately had the criminal arrested, whose name he knew from the ghost; on interrogation, this man was unable any longer to cover up his crime and confessed all. It is said that the local people were amazed when they heard about this and venerated Magistrate Lin as a godlike person, with the result that the district enjoyed peace and tranquillity.

Another incident was actually experienced by a graduate during the metropolitan examination. One night, in the examination compound, he heard the voice of a ghost. It was not just his imagination at work, for all his neighbors heard it, too. At about eight o'clock the following evening he learned that someone had died close by. Next day he handed in his paper, and just as he went out of his alley an attendant was throwing a corpse over the wall. After the examination, he met a friend who had occupied the cell next to that of the dead man, and so was able to obtain the details. The dead man was a fifty-three-year-old graduate from Kansu. After he had entered his cell, he became extremely restless, and several times sighed loudly while entreating someone, "Why do you torment me so? Can you not wait a little and let us talk it over after the examination?" On the following day the friend saw the man passing the alley. He looked haggard and seemed about to collapse. Upon returning to his cell, the man called an attendant and said, "I am already on the verge of death. I want you to call the official in charge." Hurrying on, he went into the latrine at the end of the alley and, tying his belt to a nail in the ceiling, hanged himself. Upon a piece of paper left in his cell was an account of the many evil deeds he remembered having committed. It was said that at last, during the metropolitan examination, retribution had caught up with a villain who had been fortunate enough to escape his victims' revenge during the provincial examination.

The highest-ranking man was called the "first metropolitan graduate," or *hui-yüan;* the second, *ya-k'uei;* while the sixth was known as the "head of the list," *pang-yüan,* since here, too, as in the provincial examination, the names were made public beginning with that of the sixth man. The men ranked from first to sixteenth were known as "the best," *hui-k'uei.* Although sometimes those who passed received the special title of *kung-shih,* usually they were merely admitted to the subsequent palace examination. However, since it was a rule not to fail anyone in the latter, passing the metropolitan examination was tantamount to passing the palace examination, as well.

Those who passed the metropolitan examination were delighted, of course, but they still had to go through a number of troublesome procedures before they could take the palace examination. All the passing answers were turned over to reexaminers (*fu-k'ang ta-ch'en*) especially appointed by the emperor, and in the meantime the candidates went to the Board of Rites to submit their life histories written in their own hands. The reexaminers then made certain that the calligraphy corresponded with that on the examination papers. If everything was in order they reported so to the throne, and the passing list was put into its final form.

In the metropolitan examination, also, aged candidates received special treatment. Because it would be considered an act of irreverence if an old man were to be disgraced during the palace examination, venerable scholars were excused from the latter during the Ch'ing dynasty, although earlier, in the Sung regime, men over seventy years of age frequently did participate in the palace examination. In the Ch'ing period, men over seventy who appeared for the metropolitan examination were called "aged students" (*lao-*

sheng); and even if their papers were below standard the minister of rites, as examination supervisor, petitioned the emperor to grant them nominal official rank. It is said that, as a rule, those who were eighty years of age or older received the title of professor in the Hanlin Academy, while men a hundred years of age or more were honored as assistant directors of the university. Thus the old men had the satisfaction of seeing their lifelong studies crowned with success.

The minister of rites invited candidates who were successful in the metropolitan examination, together with those who had passed it sixty years before, to a congratulatory banquet (*ch'iung-lin yen*). That festive occasion started with the lighting of incense sticks placed upon a table facing the palace. Then everyone performed the ritual of the full kowtow—three kneelings, with three full-length prostrations for each kneeling—calling out wishes for the emperor's long life. Thereupon the earthier part of the banquet could begin.

Those who passed the examination distributed printed copies of their answers (*hui-shih hei-chüan*) to relatives and friends. Inasmuch as the questions concerning the Four Books had been set by the emperor himself, the answers to this part of the examination frequently were printed. In these publications the scholar's text was preceded by an account of the author's family lineage and a name register of his relatives, and these in turn were followed by the examiners' comments. However, the happy winners of the metropolitan examination could manage to take care of this bit of modest advertising only after the palace examination had been held, since they did not have enough time to see to it between the examinations. First they faced yet another important trial.

At the beginning of the Ch'ing dynasty those scholars who had been successful in the metropolitan examination were immediately eligible for the palace examination, but during the Ch'ien-lung era still another minor prerequisite was introduced. Called the metropolitan reexamination, it served as a preparatory test for the palace examination, which was conducted by the emperor himself and which, as we have seen, no one failed. The reexamination had three purposes: it verified the adequacy of the candidates' scholarship; like the palace examination, it was held in the palace in order to familiarize the candidates with the location and to give them practice in protocol and deportment; and it afforded still another opportunity to check the identity of the candidates.

Usually the metropolitan reexamination was held on the sixteenth day of the fourth month in the Pao-ho Palace, located in about the middle of the Forbidden City, where the emperor resided. If one passed through the main gate, the Kan-men, and faced north, he would see in the square beyond the T'ai-ho Gate the T'ai-ho, Chung-ho, and Pao-ho palaces lined up in a straight row. Inside the Pao-ho Palace was a spacious hall. Measured in *chien,* the standardized distance between two of its great round pillars, the hall was nine *chien* long, from east to west, and five wide, from north to south. At the end of the hall, raised by one step, was a throne that was occupied by the emperor during great banquets and other state occasions. In this hall the candidates were seated at about three hundred desks. The palace was splendid, with a high roof; but light from the windows did not reach all the way to the center of the spacious interior.

Because the candidates were men still without status or office, they had to submit to the Board of Rites a letter of guarantee from an official stationed in the capital. It was the responsibility of this sponsor to be present when the candidates entered the hall and to verify the identity of his protégé.

As in the metropolitan examination, the examiners (*yüeh-chüan ta-ch'en*) received imperial commissions and the questions came from the emperor. But this time there was only one question on the Four Books and one poem. The examination was over in a day. The papers were checked for calligraphy against the black-ink originals that had been submitted in the metropolitan examination. If the discrepancy was too great, the candidate was summoned for interrogation; and if a substitution was uncovered the whole examination staff, from members of the Board of Rites on down, was punished. To be sure, examiners who saw only the papers were not held responsible, since they were ignorant of the circumstances; but if it turned out that the candidate's answers to previous examinations had been poor, the examiners, too, were punished.

After all the answers had been read the examiners wrote the grades on the papers and presented them to the emperor, together with the register of names. Then once again other high ministers were ordered to examine the papers. With imperial sanction, the results were announced about the eighteenth day of the fourth month. Because on this occasion the emperor was officially responsible for looking over the answers and making the decisions, the announcement of results came in the form of an imperial edict.

Candidates who finished in the first three ranks were admitted directly to the palace examination, but those in the fourth rank or lower had their right to take the examination suspended from one to three times, depending on the quality of their papers or the seriousness of their deficiencies. Of the 381 men who took the metropolitan reexamination in 1892, 283 had passed that year's metropolitan examination, but 31 had passed the one previous to that, and 4 the one before that. Those 35 men probably had been penalized by suspension. Thus, although in principle there were no failures after the metropolitan examination, in practice a man still could suffer a setback from the metropolitan reexamination, and candidates always had to be on their guard.

CHAPTER SEVEN

THE PALACE EXAMINATION
AND THE COURT REVIEW

THE ORIGIN OF THE PALACE EXAMINATION   During the T'ang dynasty the metropolitan examination, then called *kung-chü* or *li-pu shih,* the Board of Rites examination, was the final test. Those who passed it received the *chin-shih* degree and were qualified to begin an official career. Actual control over appointments and dismissals lay in the hands of the Board of Personnel, *li-pu,* which administered a placement examination, *ch'üan-shih* or *li-pu shih,* consisting of four tests. The test of the candidate's physique (*shen*) determined whether his appearance was sufficiently imposing for an official to dominate the populace, while the language test (*yen*) made sure that he did not speak with an accent and could solemnly command subordinates or deal with his equals. Both of these were personality tests reflecting the qualities stressed in the aristocratic milieu of the T'ang. The other two examinations tested skills: one in calligraphy (*shu*) determined whether the man could write a good hand; and one in composing judgments (*p'an*) ascertained his ability to formulate legal decisions without error.

Gradually this system became outdated, primarily because with the Sung dynasty and its successors the autocratic power of the emperor increased. During the time of the T'ang the metropolitan examination had been conducted by the Board of Rites, and the emperor himself was not directly involved. As a result, a personal master-disciple relationship was apt to arise between the examiner and the men he passed, and this soon developed into a bond like that between a political leader and his henchmen. In consequence, government was controlled by personal feelings rather than by concern for the general welfare, thus leading to factional strife. The situation deteriorated to the point where the cliques could not be dissolved even by the authority of the emperor. Therefore the first Sung emperor, T'ai-tsu (r. 960–76), added an additional test after the metropolitan examination. With himself as examiner, he conducted this test with the idea that thereby he would obtain the gratitude of the candidates, who would now consider him their patron, and thus develop bureaucratic solidarity. This was the origin of the regular palace examination, which was continued by later dynasties down to and including the Ch'ing.

The Board of Personnel's placement examination was continued, but its character and significance were greatly changed by the advent of the palace examination. Up through the T'ang regime the Board of Personnel was an aristocratic stronghold exercising general control over official appointments, and nepotism played a great part in promotions and demotions. Even a well-qualified man who had passed the Board of Rites examination with distinction could be failed by the Board of Personnel in the physical or language test if his parentage was undistinguished or if they did not care for his personality. In short, the system was extremely likely to lead to injustice and was an object of vigorous criticism from the rising class of scholar-officials. All this changed in the Sung period, when the aristocracy had almost entirely disappeared and the Board of Personnel became simply a bureau for managing government personnel. Although it did continue to hold the placement examination, this gradually became a mere formality; and under the Ch'ing emperors the tests of physique, language, and calligraphy, as well as the formulation of judgments, were discontinued. Therefore, his showing in the palace examination, more than anything else, determined an official's success in life.

THE DRAWING UP OF THE QUESTIONS   The palace examination was conducted by the emperor, but actually high court officials of outstanding literary ability were selected to serve as readers (*tu-chüan ta-ch'en*). Unlike their counterparts in the metropolitan examinations, these did not assign grades to the papers. That was the responsibility of the emperor, who did not actually read the answers but had the ministers do this for him and gave out grades according to their findings. There were eight of these readers, including the senior academician of the grand secretariat (*nei-ko ta-hsüeh-shih*), corresponding to a prime minister. The responsibility for this examination was not confined to one department of government, but officials from its different branches were called upon as needed. For example, censors—who performed some of the functions of prosecuting attorneys and were not linked organizationally to the secretariat— were placed in charge of the supervision of the examination, while even eunuchs worked at odd jobs in the palace in connection with this examination.

On the day before the examination, the readers presented drafts of their questions to the throne and, after obtaining imperial approval, turned them over to the grand secretariat for printing. To prevent leaks or thefts, soldiers stood an all-night guard around the secretariat. Meanwhile the Board of Rites was charged with the printing of the answer booklets. These had covers with spaces on them for the candidate's name, age, and family background, followed by sixteen pages, each with six vertical lines printed in red. The rule required that the candidate write only twenty-four characters in a row, but inasmuch as the pages bore no horizontal lines each candidate had to decide the spacing for himself. The outer margin was delineated by a thick red line. Beautifully printed on paper of high quality, the answer booklets were superb pieces of craftsmanship. They were distributed, one to each candidate, on the day of the examination, together with draft paper. In addition, the officials of the Board of Rites had to make arrangements with the grand chamberlain, go to the Pao-ho Palace, set up desks for the candidates, and attach the seat numbers to the desks.

ENTERING THE EXAMINATION HALL   Early in the morning of the twenty-first day of the fourth month the candidates passed through the main palace gate, the Wu-men, or Meridian Gate, and assembled in front of the T'ai-ho Gate, which rose straight ahead. Usually this gate was kept closed and only the side portals on the east and west (*chao-te men* and *chen-tu men*) were open. The candidates were divided into two groups: those assigned to odd-numbered seats went to the east gate for their roll call, and those assigned to even-numbered desks went to the west portal. When the roll call, conducted by officials from the Board of Rites, was completed, the answer papers were distributed and each group passed through its designated gate and entered the plaza in front of the T'ao-ho Palace. Brushes, inkstones, and other articles brought by the candidates were carried for them by soldiers on duty, since as imperial guests the scholars had to be treated with the utmost courtesy.

Still divided into two groups, the candidates crossed the plaza and, after passing through small gates on the east and west (*chung-tso men* and *chung-yu men*), climbed a broad terrace enclosed by a triple railing and paved with cut stone, beyond which soared the Pao-ho Palace. The two groups of candidates came together at the center of the terrace, where a magnificent marble ramp led to the main palace entrance. Dragons were embossed upon the marble of the ramp to make it less slippery. To be sure, this "dragon stairway" was reserved for the emperor's sole use; his subjects used the stairs to the right and to the left.

At the top of the ramp, under the curving eaves of the palace, an incense table had been set up. When the candidates had finished lining up on the terrace below, the senior academician of the grand secretariat appeared beneath the eaves at the east, bearing a packet containing the printed examination papers. He was greeted by the minister of rites, who knelt to receive the parcel, placed it upon the table, and bowed, touching his head to the floor three times. After that the master of ceremonies led the examination officials, from readers on down, to the table, where he lined them up to perform the full kowtow in unison at his command. Next it was the candidates' turn to do the same, again at the command of the master of ceremonies. Then officials from the Board of Rites opened the packet, took out the papers, and gave one to each of the candidates waiting at the bottom of the ramp. They accepted them respectfully after bowing three times. Guided by the master of ceremonies, the candidates then went up the stairs, entered the palace, and seated themselves at the designated desks. They were followed by the soldiers carrying their belongings. The soldiers deposited these at the owner's desks, after which they immediately withdrew. Thereupon the examination began.

THE FORM OF THE ANSWERS   Because the emperor himself was the all-responsible official for the palace examination, the form of the questions differed from that of earlier examinations in that they were cast in the style of an imperial rescript. When the *kung-shih* opened their question sheets they saw that the questions were exceedingly long and written in a most solemn style. As proper form required, the questions began with words to this effect: "You graduates are talented men who have qualified in repeated examinations and now, facing the palace examination, are about to try to answer My questions. I am the Son of Heaven, responsible for governing the Empire. Night and day I rack My brains so that the people will be able to live in tranquillity. Fortunately I have this opportunity to pose questions to you graduates and I wish to hear your well-considered opinions upon the following." Then the questions were presented, and after them came the concluding instructions: "At this fine opportunity, express yourselves frankly without fearing anyone! If you have reservations, or flinch, or do not write completely what you think, or try to fulfill your responsibilities through flattering words which in your heart you do not mean, then you will be going against My will."

Since they were submitting their opinions upon the imperial questions, the candidates' answers were written in the form of a memorial, beginning with "Your humble servant replies to Your question; Your humble servant has heard." This formula was followed by an introduction, generally to this effect: "Without a pause in state affairs, Your Majesty devotes Yourself to government, and I am most gratefully fortunate that, despite this, You take time from the pressure of work to seek from even one as inexperienced as Your servant his opinions on the rights and wrongs of past and present governments." Then they began the actual texts of their answers.

Each line of the answer sheet held twenty-four characters, but the candidates left blank the top two spaces, in order to allow room for such terms as "The Emperor, Your Majesty," which had to be raised above the rest of the text at the top of a new line whenever they occurred in the answer. Also it was customary to write the first character, "Your humble servant," in a slightly smaller size and a little to the right. In addition, there were a number of other regulations, including some concerning the use of raised characters (*t'ai-tzu*). Words designating the emperor himself or matters directly relating to the emperor, such as "the Imperial Countenance" or "the Imperial Decree," had to be written two spaces above the text. However, still more elevated in Chinese eyes than the emperor were his parents and ancestors, and words designating them were raised three spaces above the text, even though they jutted into the margin. Terms associated with the emperor, such as "the capital," "the palace," and "the state," were raised one space.

Raising these characters here and there served to break the monotony of the text, since page after page of writing with two spaces left blank at the top of each line was regarded as unsightly. Generally, "The Emperor, Your Majesty" appeared in the fifth or ninth line, and the term had to be repeated two lines later. Furthermore, the first mention of "The Emperor, Your Majesty" had to be preceded by "I respectfully consider," which had to occur right at the bottom of the preceding line, without any character or empty space following it. An empty space at the end of a line was also considered to be unsightly, and the key to composing a correct answer lay in making a careful count of one's characters before coming to an elevated term. Fortunately, in the classical Chinese language there are convenient particles that, carefully used, make it possible to comply with this form. An empty space at the end of a line was not a formal offense, but it did incur a demerit.

Since the questions set by the emperor were quite long, the answers had to be of a certain length. One employing less than a thousand characters was not acceptable, and it was a rule not to pass such papers. At the beginning of the Ch'ing dynasty the emperor's questions concerned the candidate's opinions about the actual problems of ruling the country, but gradually they became formalized and called only for the candidates' views on ideological questions concerning historical events. However, on their part the candidates were well acquainted with the literary sources relating to these events and, since they had to write answers demonstrating their own erudition, could not submit "empty" answers devoid of content.

There was also a set form for the conclusion of the answer: "I, Your humble servant, a superficial scholar newly advanced, not realizing where I was, have ventured to state my own views and am so ashamed of offending the Majesty of the Emperor that I do not know where to hide. I respectfully submit my answer." It was considered clever to leave fourteen empty lines after this concluding sentence, but a government order stated that this elegant touch was not mandatory.

Since in principle the palace examination was given by the emperor himself, there was all the difference in the world between the polite treatment the graduates received on that occasion and the abuse meted out to them during previous examinations. This time, examination clerks and eunuchs served them tea and a meal at noon. Because the interior of the palace was rather dark and daylight did not penetrate all the way into the great hall, men sitting in the shadow of a pillar were allowed to move nearer the windows.

The answers had to be completed by sunset. Incomplete papers were failed, and it happened that those who were slow could not finish in the dark. However, since this was the last and critical time for the graduates, men often frantically held onto their answer sheets. Thus, in 1899 Chang Chien-hsün, a graduate from Kwangsi, had completed all but the last page of his paper at sunset. When a member of the staff came to look, he saw that what Chang had written was really excellent. Out of sympathy he carried Chang's desk into the light beyond the door and allowed him to write under the eaves. The candidate, a man from the country, became very excited and so completely lost his head that the final part was written in a pitifully confused hand. The staff member thought it was utterly bad, but since the entire answer had been completed, he collected it together with the other papers and passed it on to the readers. And lo and behold, Chang's paper came in first.

As has been indicated, deep in the interior of the Pao-ho Palace was the emperor's throne. During this examination he was supposed to show himself and review the candidates, but few emperors did this very diligently. Especially during the late Ch'ing period, the emperor scarcely ever appeared at an examination, and the atmosphere seems to have become lax and the occasion to have lost its air of gravity. It is said that the soldiers detailed as porters did not help the candidates at all but merely stood off to one side, watching them painfully dragging their heavy belongings. In earlier times, by contrast, as in the Sung period, emperors were extraordinarily enthusiastic and really did appear at the palace examination.

About a thousand years ago, when Emperor T'ai-tsung (r. 976–98) of the Sung personally conducted a palace examination, one of the officials in attendance, Wang Yü-ch'eng (954–1001) described the scene in a poem, which included these lines:

> Until dusk the emperor remains in the Chin-luan Palace.
> The willows of the palace hang deeply in the third-month mist.
> The scent of burning incense flies into a thousand inkstones.
> The graduates' linen robes are shining white as snow.

Because most candidates were entering the Imperial Palace for the first time when they took this ultimate examination, they put on brand-new clothes, glowing as white as snow. It may have been a tranquil scene to others, but the candidates themselves were nervous, for they knew that they might be eliminated still. For them it was a time to work with all their might.

CORRECTING THE ANSWERS   The answer papers, with the names of their authors covered, were delivered to the high officials serving as readers, who had gathered in the Wen-hua Hall within the palace. If there were eight readers, each man received thirty or forty papers, which were dealt out in sequence, one at a time, like playing cards, although out of mercy aged ministers were dealt a smaller stack. Each man then inspected his share of answers and assigned them preliminary grades. This preliminary grading was extremely important because, even though the opinions of the examiners might differ, as a general rule they did not give grades that were too far apart.

Depending upon the grades they received, papers were divided into five groups. An empty circle designated full credit; a filled-in circle, eighty percent; a triangle, sixty percent; a line, forty percent; and an X, twenty percent. Above the grade the examiner wrote his name, thus clearly taking responsibility for it. Once read, a paper was sent to the next man. After all eight readers had graded it, the results were totaled. It is said that this work alone took three days.

Since the examiners were great ministers trusted by the emperor, at the beginning of the Ch'ing dynasty they were permitted to return home after each day's work. Later, however, after the Ch'ien-lung era, they had to sleep in small rooms located on either side of the Wen-hua Hall in order to prevent any dishonesty.

From among several hundred papers the examiners had to select the ten best answers, rank them provisionally, and present them to the emperor for his decision. This process of selection was always a source of trouble, however, because each examiner tried to have the ten papers chosen from among those he had graded first and wanted these to be assigned a high rank. To select one paper from each examiner did not solve the problem, since there was the danger that a number of good papers might be excluded if they had been assigned to the same man. Furthermore, the elderly examination chairman, as a rule, received a small number of papers to grade, but it did happen that a disproportionate number of his papers were favored. All this led to intense disputes among fellow readers.

Inasmuch as the papers were literary exercises, the grading could not be completely just. In search of objective standards, readers shifted their attention from examining the content of the answers to concentrating upon style, and finally upon calligraphy. Furthermore, calligraphy itself was not valued aesthetically: the "square writing" style, bereft of all individuality, in which the characters were made to resemble those used in printer's type, inevitably received good marks because it was pleasing to look at. If famous calligraphers, such as Wang Hsi-chih (321–79), had tried to take the palace examination during the Ch'ing dynasty, they would have failed it completely.

During the late Ch'ing period, in order to prevent disputes among the examiners, the decision was entrusted entirely to one elderly chairman. But it is said that, under this system, only papers that received full credit from all the readers were selected for inclusion among the top ten.

Early in the morning of the twenty-fourth day of the fourth month, the examiners delivered the ten best papers to the emperor, while their authors waited outside for an audience. The emperor himself examined the ten papers and ranked them. Generally, he followed the order in which they had been arranged by the readers, but sometimes there were unexpected surprises. Usually the answer papers were presented to the emperor with the seals opened and the candidates' names revealed; but some emperors ordered that they be submitted with the seals intact. It also happened that an emperor assigned grades after looking at the candidates' faces and made his decision after carefully scrutinizing their behavior and appearance. In other cases, emperors scolded the readers for bad judgment and for having graded answers according to their own ideas. Some emperors, feeling a need for self-assertion but finding it difficult to conduct a real investigation, picked the top man arbitrarily and then ranked the others. Whatever he did, the emperor was absolutely free to do as he wished, and without restraint, since after the Sung dynasty China's emperors were despots in all matters.

For everyone the most important problem was to determine which candidates would be ranked first, second, and third, because the first three places constituted the top group, *chia*, towering high above all others. The man who came in fourth and the others lumped in the second group were considered merely to have done relatively well and did not receive any special privileges.

AN ILLITERATE CHAIRMAN   The readers for the palace examination usually were appointed from among especially learned high officials, and being selected for this duty gave a man much prestige. Yet here, too, there were occasional exceptions. One of these was the Manchu general Chao-hui (1708–64), who was selected as examination chairman by Emperor Ch'ien-lung.

In 1760, General Chao-hui crushed the extremely fierce Ölöd (or Eleuth) in Sinkiang, secured the southern T'ien-shan route, and celebrated a magnificent and imposing triumph upon returning to Peking. Very pleased, Ch'ien-lung appointed him to be examination chairman for the following year. Chao-hui, much surprised, tried to decline: "This is an absurd order. For a battle I would hasten anywhere, but examinations are really my weak point. Please appoint someone else."

The emperor responded, "I know that you do not know how to read, but you are supposed to be able to write your name."

"Since it is necessary for battle reports, I can write my name after a fashion."

"That is fine. Have the others read the papers first, and then grade them last yourself. If a paper has many empty circles, you add one too; if a paper has many triangles, add your triangle. Then write your name on the paper. The others will take care of the rest."

Thus the illiterate Chao-hui ended up as chief reader. Among the graduates that year was Chao I (1708–64), later famous as a historian. The examiners selected Chao I for first place, but when Emperor Ch'ien-lung looked over their list he noticed that a Wang Chieh from Shensi was ranked third. Because during the war a year earlier Shensi had been on the route traversed by many soldiers and horses, and the emperor knew that the people had made great sacrifices, he gave Wang Chieh first place and ranked Chao I third. This was done because achieving a first caused great rejoicing among the people of the man's home area, who shared in his glory.

On the other hand Chao I, relegated to third place, was extremely disappointed and depressed. Before the examination he had worked for the central government as a man qualified for temporary employment, had been treated affectionately by the officials, who had praised his abilities, and had anticipated an outstanding career. After this experience with the imperial will, however, he gradually withdrew from government and earnestly turned to scholarship, taking a special interest in history. The fame of his *Nien-erh-shih-cha-chi* is still unequaled today, and his many other works were also acclaimed by later scholars. Probably no one who has devoted himself to Chinese history has not benefited from Chao I's work. This must be called a great achievement by accident, and as a result his influence upon later generations was much greater than it would have been had he become just another statesman.

In the early Ch'ing dynasty the readers of examinations, as their title indicates, actually read the answers to the emperor. This custom began earlier, however, inasmuch as during the Sung period, too, examiners selected outstanding answers to palace examinations and took turns reading them to the emperor. During the long reign of Sung Emperor Jen-tsung (1023–64) an official named Wang Mien frequently served as examiner for palace examinations. He read so beautifully, in his clear voice, that the emperor always liked the papers he presented and gave them high marks. Graduates are said to have prayed that their papers would be read by him.

ANNOUNCEMENT OF THE RESULTS   On the day after the emperor had ranked the ten best papers, the results were made public. Since this was an examination conducted by the emperor, a simple announcement would not suffice. Instead a splendid ceremony was held for an occasion that bestowed the status of scholar upon those men of merit. It was termed the "calling of names," *ch'uan-lu* or *ch'ang-ming*, because in the presence of the emperor each man's name was called out individually. Like an English or American commencement exercise, it was both a graduation terminating many years spent as a student and a coming-of-age ceremony marking the attainment of the qualification to be a self-supporting official.

The ceremony took place on the twenty-fifth day of the fourth month in the T'ai-ho Pavilion, the largest and most important in the palace, where all important formal ceremonies were held. On that day officials serving in Peking attended in ceremonial dress, gathering on the terrace before the pavilion, while those of noble rank climbed the stairs and took their places below the eaves. The successful candidates, each wearing a hat decorated with a *san-chih chiu-yeh ting*, a "three branches and nine leaves button" resembling a halberd, were placed to the rear of the hundreds of officials, who were lined up in all their dignity.

When these preparations were completed the emperor, followed by attendants, emerged from his residence as bells and drums were sounded from the top of the Wu-men, the Meridian Gate of the palace. Music played while the emperor entered the T'ai-ho Pavilion but stopped as soon as he mounted the throne. When the master of ceremonies snapped a whip with a leather thong three times, the music started once more and the readers advanced to perform the full kowtow, after which the music again ceased.

Then the premier came forth under the eastern gable, holding a board upon which was pasted the list of names of the qualifying men, and kneeling before the minister of rites, presented it to him. Because the list bore the imperial seal it was referred to as the "golden placard," *chin-pang*, or "imperial placard," *huang-pang*. The minister, having received the carefully prepared placard, rose to his feet, placed the list upon a specially prepared table, bowed over it three times, and retired. Then, with stately music playing, the court master of ceremonies conducted the qualifying candidates to a place in front of the hundreds of officials. At the call for "profound obeisance" the graduates knelt as one man. While the music halted temporarily the master of ceremonies, standing a little to the east of the eaves, read out the imperial decree. Generally it went something like this: "Because you graduates, coming from afar, took the palace examination and qualified brilliantly, We are greatly satisfied. Therefore, because We bestow on you the degree of *chin-shih*, from now on increasingly strive to be truly loyal."

Then the calling of the names began. At the call of "the first man of the first group, Mr. So-and-so," repeated three times, the master of ceremonies himself sought out the man, brought him to the front of the group, and bade him kneel at a place slightly east of the great pavilion's center. Then the second man was called forth and placed slightly west of center, and the third man was positioned behind the first. After that the names of all the candidates in the second group were called out, followed by those in the third and last group, but the men of these groups remained in place.

After the calling of names the music started up again, somewhat more lively than before. When the master of ceremonies gave the command for the most solemn rite of all, the graduates—now, with their degrees, officials at the beginning of their honored careers—performed the full kowtow in unison. When this obeisance was over, the master of ceremonies led the new *chin-shih* back to their places to the rear of all the older officials.

Once more the music stopped, and at a signal from the master of ceremonies the minister of rites respectfully raised the imperial placard bearing the names of the *chin-shih*, descended the central steps, and placed it upon a litter called the "cloud vessel," *yün-p'an*. Preceded by a yellow umbrella (that being the imperial color), the "cloud vessel" was carried through the main gate of the palace. The minister himself and the first three graduates followed it on foot, while the other *chin-shih* departed through the east and west gates. When the master of ceremonies snapped his whip three times and the music recommenced, the emperor descended from the throne to return to his residence. When the music ceased altogether, the officials, too, left as a group. With that the great ceremony came to an end.

The three groups of graduates were given somewhat different *chin-shih* degrees: *chin-shih chi-ti, chin-shih ch'u-sheng,* and *t'ung chin-shih ch'u-sheng.* In the West *chin-shih,* literally "presented scholar," has often been translated as "doctor." The three men in the first group, the *chuang-yüan, pang-yen,* and *t'an-hua,* were greatly honored, and, of course, the first man achieved the greatest glory.

When the procession arrived in front of the Meridian Gate, the placard was laid in a five-colored sedan chair called the "dragon arbor," *lung-t'ing,* and, carried by soldiers and accompanied by musicians, was paraded through the town. Eventually it was set down outside the East Ch'ang-an Gate, east of the T'ien-an Portal and beside the road leading from the Imperial City and T'ien-an Square into the Inner City of Peking. The new *chin-shih* also gathered there in order to take a good look at their names on the list. During the great ceremony at the palace they had been in a dreamlike trance, but by this time they had recovered their senses and were filled with indescribable emotion. For three days the placard was posted outside the gate, displayed to the crowds that came to see it. Then it was sent to the archives (*nei-ko*) for safekeeping.

The new *chin-shih* had been accompanied to the East Ch'ang-an Gate by the parading soldiers and musicians, but these now dispersed. The three top men only were taken by the capital prefect to the prefectural hall for a congratulatory banquet. There, the top man took the seat of honor, facing south, with the second man on his left and the third on his right. The prefect, acting as host, took the lowest seat. Music for the occasion was provided by singing girls from the palace studio. After the banquet, the prefect and subprefect accompanied only the first man back to his residence. That young man, who yesterday had been nothing more than an inconsequential student, today was an altogether eminent personage.

Afterward, at least for a while, the new *chin-shih* did not have a day without a private or public banquet, a ceremony, or the like. They were so happily occupied that they could have shouted for joy. So did they prove the truth of the old saying that, ever since the days of antiquity, has told of the four occasions that are the high points in a man's life:

> Sweet rain after a long drought.
> Meeting an old friend in a strange place.
> The wedding night in the nuptial chamber.
> The sight of one's name on the golden placard.

THE OFFICIAL BANQUET AND CEREMONY TO EXPRESS THANKS The day after the palace ceremony the new *chin-shih* received an invitation from the Board of Rites to attend a congratulatory banquet. Although this took place at the board, a high official from the inner court acted as host because it was donated by the emperor. It was a great feast, attended by the administrative staff as well as by the palace examination readers. At the tables officials and new *chin-shih* were mixed appropriately, but this time the seats of honor were occupied by the ministers and high officials because the banquet was given to thank them for their trouble. Since it was presented by the emperor the food and wine came from the palace, music was provided by singing girls from the imperial studio, and the master of ceremonies went among the guests, pouring wine.

A strange custom was associated with this banquet. When it was ended, and the real guests were leaving, menials who had been on watch at the door rushed into the hall and openly gathered up the leftovers. Shouting and struggling among themselves, they created a great uproar. The *chin-shih* could only look on in blank amazement and, while trying to protect their clothing from gravy and other food stains, make their way out of the hall, utterly disconcerted. Witnessing this breach in official discipline must have made a deep impression on those young men, still only officials in embryo. This upsetting tradition had been established by the beginning of the Ch'ing regime. Emperor Yung-cheng (r. 1723–36), famous for tightening discipline, issued a strict order forbidding it, but despite his decree it continued unchanged to the end of the dynasty.

Four days later, on the twenty-eighth day of the fourth month, the new *chin-shih* proceeded in a group to the Meridian Gate of the palace and made obeisance from afar toward the imperial residence in a ceremony intended to convey their gratitude for their degrees and the banquet. At this time the top man had to offer a written expression of gratitude on behalf of the whole group; but usually, because he was not yet familiar with the forms proper to a *chin-shih*, he asked a senior to write it for him, generally the top man of three years earlier. If the latter was away from the capital on official business or otherwise unavailable, the man from the year before substituted for him. If this man also was unavailable, there was a great commotion to find someone who had graduated as one of the three top men. The new man might go around from person to person, being refused each time with a "So-and-so would be good," only to end up with the very official he had asked at the start. These men were exceedingly hesitant to undertake the task of drawing up a document in the complicated official language, and also hesitant about accepting the large gift of money that it entailed. Thus, immediately after obtaining his degree the top man had a memorable lesson in the difficulties of getting along in the official world.

On the appointed day the top man led the other new degree-holders to the place in front of the Meridian Gate where the master of ceremonies eagerly awaited them. There they lined up in two groups on opposite sides of the avenue. The top man came forward to present his memorial, placed it upon a table prepared in advance, then withdrew. Obeying the directions of the master of ceremonies, all the *chin-shih* turned in unison toward the north to perform the full kowtow at the command, "Profound obeisance." At this time it was customary for the emperor to present each man with clothing, caps, shoes, and other gifts, as well as with five ounces of silver. The memorial of the *chin-shih* was forwarded to the Board of Rites and from there to the archives for safekeeping.

On the first day of the fifth month the new *chin-shih* were ordered to pay their respects in the temple of Confucius located in the university. Again the top man, together with the two other members of the first group, played the leading role, bowing to the statue of Confucius and presenting offerings, then proceeding to the images of Yen-tzu, Tzu-ssu, Tseng-tzu, Mencius, and other Confucian worthies, which were ranged along the sides. The libationer (*chi-chiu*) and the tutor (*ssu-yeh*) of the university gave a simple reception known as the "ceremony of casting off rough clothing," *shih-ho,* which is to say, the ceremony of reporting that one had risen from student to official status.

After that the Board of Rites memorialized the emperor, requesting that a commemorative stele (*t'i-ming pei*) be set up in front of the university. It was customary for the Board of Works to spend a hundred ounces of silver upon the project. The names of all the *chin-shih* from that year's class, from the first to the last man, were engraved upon the face of a large stone. This tradition began in the time of the Yüan dynasty, and since the site of the university did not change after that, steles ranging from the Yüan to the late Ch'ing period were lined up like gravestones in a cemetery. Even so, because some Ch'ing officials pocketed part of the government funds by arranging to efface the carvings on steles from earlier times and re-use the stones, it is believed that some records from the Yüan and Ming periods were lost.

To enable the new *chin-shih* to set up triumphal arches in front of their residences, the government issued eighty ounces of silver to the one who had finished in first place and thirty ounces each to the others in the group. These arches were similar to Japanese *torii* made of stone. If no suitable space was available in front of a *chin-shih's* house, it was erected at the entrance to the lane leading to his home. Not all *chin-shih* actually built these arches, but often, for the sake of the reputation of the town or village, the people of his home area assisted a top man to set up a magnificent arch. Some of these arches can be seen still in various parts of China.

To commemorate the great occasion of the palace examination a written record, *teng-k'o lu* or *chin-pang t'i-ming lu,* was compiled in the Board of Rites. First appeared the "decree," that is, the questions issued by the emperor; then the "memorials," that is, the answers of the top three men; and finally the names and native places of all the *chin-shih.* This record was presented to the emperor and, in printed form, was distributed to all government offices throughout the country.

Sometimes individual *chin-shih* published their answers at their own expense and presented them to relatives and friends. In such a case, rather than use the answers they had written for the palace examination, they printed the answers to the questions on the Four Books they had given in the metropolitan examination. They made this substitution because the palace examination answers were written as memorials to the emperor, which theoretically should not be made public, and also because they were formal exercises relatively uninteresting in content. However, "memorial arch bookstores" are said to have competed to obtain the original palace examination answers in order to print and sell them at great profit to graduates of the metropolitan examination, who still faced the palace examination.

THE CHIN-SHIH DURING THE T'ANG DYNASTY   So far we have considered the examination system as it existed in its most complex form in the late Ch'ing period. This system differed in some ways from that of about a thousand years earlier, when, during the T'ang dynasty, the hereditary aristocracy was still flourishing. Now let us look at the examination system of that period, inasmuch as T'ang precedents were extraordinarily influential in later times.

During the T'ang dynasty the capital was at Ch'ang-an, in modern Shensi. Because the palace examination had not yet been introduced, the *chin-shih* was awarded directly after the T'ang equivalent of the metropolitan examination, the *kung-chü.* Even so, the joy of the men when they reached this final stage and achieved the glory of being a *chin-shih* was just as great as that of their successors in later dynasties. Since aristocratic values still survived in the T'ang period, certain refinements were still practiced.

After the announcement of the names of those who had qualified by examination, all the successful *chin-shih* went to the house of the examiner (*chih kung-chü*) to express their gratitude. Since there were so many of them they met in the garden, and each man introduced himself, giving his name, seat number, and age. Thus they entered into a master-disciple covenant with the examiner and swore a lifelong oath of friendship. If one of the new *chin-shih* had had the same seat number as that held by the examiner when he won his degree, he was received with special favor as one who had assumed the mantle of the older man. When this general gathering ended, the top man only was invited into the examiner's house, to sit down to a private reception. After that the examiner took the men to call at the house of the chief minister and introduced them individually. Then for the first time the new *chin-shih* entered into the world of aristocratic society. Those who became *chin-shih* in the same year called each other "classmate," associated as comrades, and helped each other in times of need.

Next the new *chin-shih* gathered in an official banquet hall, Ch'i-chi Yüan, for a congratulatory feast. This banquet hall was famous at the time for serving the best food and drink in Ch'ang-an. Then the new *chin-shih* were examined by the Board of Rites, which administered the tests of physique, language, calligraphy, and skill in composing judgments that have been described earlier in this chapter. Those who qualified received their official assignments immediately. After this series of tests, sometimes known as "closing tests," *kuan-shih*, there was another great feast, called the "closing banquet," *kuan-yen*. This celebration was held beside the Serpentine (Chü-chiang), a lake in the southeastern part of the capital, and there the men played a game of floating wine goblets upon the water. Because the *chin-shih* were about to depart for distant posts, this was also a leave-taking feast, so it was called a "farewell banquet," *li-yen*.

In the neighborhood of the Serpentine were banquet grounds maintained by the several government bureaus, and high officials brought their families along to participate in this celebration. Some officials brought their marriageable daughters, considering this a good occasion to choose a son-in-law. Not only high officials but the emperor himself went to a restaurant called the Purple Cloud Pavilion, Tzu-yün Lou, to watch the spectacle. From this two-storied building the emperor most likely took pleasure in the scene of the officials and the new *chin-shih* dressed up to express their exultation and high spirits, passing back and forth and, after the banquet, playing a mounted game resembling polo.

Two of the youngest and most handsome of the new *chin-shih* were chosen to "look for flowers" (*t'an hua,* the term later used to denote the third-highest graduate). They went through all of Ch'ang-an's famous parks, picked the most beautiful bloom of the tree peony they could find, and exhibited it. If someone else came up with a still more beautiful tree peony blossom, the first two men had to drink a "penalty goblet." When the celebration was over, all the new *chin-shih* mounted horses and went to admire the place from which the day's flowers had come. For the new *chin-shih* it was the best day of their lives. After having worn their nerves thin during the long arduous trials of an examination-taker, suddenly, as *chin-shih,* they found a bright future stretching out before them. The consecutive celebrations had filled them with joy, and they felt that now they had reached the pinnacle of happiness. At last they were rewarded for long years of toil. Many joyful poems concerning this occasion have come down to us. This one, written by Meng Chiao (751–814), was long popular in China:

> The drudgery of yesterday now is not worth a sigh.
> Today the prospects are vast, my heart is full of deep emotion.
> The spring breeze blows, I have passed, the horse's hooves
>   are light.
> A whole day I have spent viewing Ch'ang-an's flowers.

North of the Serpentine stood the Tz'u-en Monastery, founded by the famous pilgrim-monk Hsüan-tsang, with its great soaring Wild Goose Pagoda. Perhaps in the beginning the new *chin-shih* themselves wrote their names on its walls, but later they chose an outstanding calligrapher from their group to do this. Still later the names were engraved with a chisel so that they could not be effaced easily. It was customary also for a man when he became a chief minister or a great general to return to the pagoda and fill in his name with vermilion ink. In Yüan and later times, commemorative steles were set up before the temple of Confucius.

THE HONORS AND RESPONSIBILITIES OF THE TOP CHIN-SHIH   The top man was treated far better than the others. If he was single, he constantly received offers from influential and high-ranking officials to take one of their daughters in marriage. Some powerful men even tried to force a married first-place graduate to divorce the wife who had shared his years of poverty and become their son-in-law instead. This is the theme of the famous drama *Lute Song,* written by Kao Ming, who lived at the end of the Yüan period and in the early Ming years. Its main character is Ts'ai Yung, a first-place graduate of the Later Han period (although this is a case of poetic license, since at that time the examination system had not yet been developed). And it tells the story of how Ts'ai Yung, although he already had a loving wife, was forced by order of the powerful Chief Minister Niu to become his son-in-law.

A first-place *chin-shih* also appears in *A Dream at Han-tan*, written by T'ang Hsien-tsu (1550–1616). This story was famous not only in China but also in Japan, where a well-known play was derived from it. The plot tells how, in the thriving city of Han-tan, Lu Sheng, a poor young man, borrowed a pillow from a wizard and, while drowsing, saw his whole life in a dream. This vision began with his attaining his heart's desire and receiving the *chin-shih* degree in first place. Then he performed great deeds as a general, but as soon as he had returned home in triumph, he was slandered and condemned to death. When it became clear that the accusations were false he was appointed chief minister and was about to attain a perfect death when he awoke to find himself, poor as before, beneath the eaves of an inn, with the millet he was cooking about ready to eat. Then Lu Sheng realized that human life is as fleeting as a dream and became a disciple of the wizard to learn his arts.

Thus did the world honor a first-place *chin-shih*, but his responsibilities too were heavy. *Chin-shih* received unequaled honors from the emperor so that in times of emergency they would be the pillars of the dynasty. Because the top man received such exceptional honors, his obligations were even greater, and he had to prepare himself to lay down his life for the emperor without regret. In the last years of the Southern Sung period, when the capital had fallen to the Mongols and it was clear that the dynasty was doomed, Chief Minister Wen T'ien-hsiang, a first-place *chin-shih,* led the Sung's few remaining troops to battle in many places, and eventually gave his life for the Chinese people or, rather, for the emperor. His poem about the Sea of Solitude, Ling-ting Yang, in the Gulf of Kwangtung well expresses the position of a first-place graduate:

> My encounter with suffering began with my studies.
> Four long years I have passed in warfare.
> Mountains and rivers destroyed, fluff blown by
>   the wind.
> A whole lifetime of ups and downs, blown around
>   like duckweed.
> By Fearsome Rapids I expressed my fears.
> In the Sea of Solitude I lament my solitude.

> Human life always ends in death.
> My true heart will illuminate history.

This is the poem of a man who has remained undaunted despite many defeats, has accepted all hardships ever since he began his studies, and has gained a bitter wisdom after a long life.

A HANDSOME YOUTH OF FIFTY YEARS AGO To become a *chin-shih* was considered the hardest of hard tasks. Often, while a man persevered, absorbed in his studies for the examinations, the years passed before he was aware of their loss, and he who had been a rosy-cheeked youth became an old man of fifty or sixty years without realizing what had happened to him. Already in the T'ang period there was a saying, "One who becomes a *chin-shih* at fifty is still comparatively young."

At the beginning of the Sung period, when after the palace examination the names of the successful men were being called out, the emperor noticed among the new *chin-shih* a white-haired old man who turned out to be seventy-three years of age. To the emperor's inquiry about his children the man replied that he was single, whereupon the emperor in sympathy gave him a beautiful palace lady as wife. Some of the wits of the day quickly made fun of him:

> The groom telling the bride his age:
> Fifty years ago twenty three.

There was also a man named Chan I who, after obtaining the *chin-shih*, composed a poem making fun of himself:

> Having read five or six loads of books,
> When old I obtained my official gown.
> The beauty asked how old I am:
> Fifty years ago twenty-three.

AFTER TRIUMPH, FAILURE Receiving a first place did not assure a man of an untroubled official career or of rapid promotion. By no means did all the first-place men end as generals or chief ministers. Attaining first place in life was not simply a matter of ability, for luck played an important part; and a man who had been lucky once might yet be deserted by fortune and fall back into the ranks, if not into ignominy.

Lung An-yen, the top man in 1814, had come to the attention of Emperor Chia-ch'ing (r. 1796–1821) because he was a protégé of a high Manchu official, and thus became a top *chin-shih* through luck rather than ability. The emperor was very trusting and had been upset when Lung's name did not appear among the top three candidates. Hearing rumors to this effect, the readers in the next palace examination recommended him for first place, thus pleasing the emperor, who readily gave his official approval. He had Lung assigned to the bureau responsible for compiling the *Shih-lu*, the "veritable records" of the preceding reign. However, Lung's wife was so jealous that there was always trouble at home, and sometimes he stayed away from his house. Once, while he was gone, a messenger from the *Shih-lu* Compilation Bureau brought a document that needed revision. But Lung was in no hurry to go home, and while he was still absent a second messenger came. His wife, who had not had a chance to show the document to her husband, gave it unrevised to the messenger. Unfortunately there was an important passage in the document and Lung's not having examined it led to a serious error that immediately cost him his prestigious position. During the reign of the succeeding emperor, Tao-kuang (1821–51), Lung An-yen was pardoned and reinstated in a low position. But his career had suffered a lasting blow, and since he had no special abilities, he ended as an undistinguished petty official, sad testimony to the fact that a position won by good luck can easily be lost by bad.

Fewer first-place *chin-shih* than we might expect succeeded in becoming chief ministers. The fortunes of other *chin-shih* also varied, and the glory of the degree for which they had struggled half their lives sometimes turned out to be surprisingly elusive. The mental state of an unfortunate old official must have been quite complicated. Especially when he saw younger men hard at work upon their studies, he was at a loss whether to encourage them or to dampen their zeal. Chao Ch'ung of the Sung dynasty expressed his feelings in a poem:

> In old age the ambition for fame fades.
> Alone on a thin horse I ride in the country.
> In a solitary village a lamp burns until dawn.
> I know someone is studying the night through.

An examination-taker might reply that going through the examinations produced a certain amount of despair but that not taking them caused a man to sink all the deeper into despair. Thus, young men were determined to succeed, and old officials echoed their sentiments, honoring the spirit of perseverance, no matter how difficult the ordeal.

A SHORTCUT EVEN IN THE PALACE EXAMINATION   Because this was an examination that stressed form more than anything else, and the content of the initial section of fourteen lines (*ts'e-mao*) was set, it was possible to plan this introduction ahead of time. Acquaintances of an examiner, therefore, wrote out this opening section and sent it to him, requesting him to edit it. In effect, this device actually amounted to a request that the examiner later recall the opening passage and give the paper a good grade. Each candidate felt that since everyone did this he would be harmed unless he did it too, and thus he busily hunted up connections who could help him. Things appeared to be fair on the surface, but at least one reader was sure to know the identity of a candidate; and the only difference was between those who would say so and those who kept quiet. Naturally, knowing the authorship of the papers led to inequities, but the readers also realized that gross unfairness on their part would immediately be conspicuous. Furthermore, it was a special feature of this examination that the examiners did not have ultimate responsibility for decisions but were overshadowed in this by the emperor.

During the reign of Emperor Hsien-feng (1851–62) the imperial relative Su Shun exercised great influence, interfered in domestic affairs and foreign relations, and was greatly hated by Chinese officials. At the palace examination of 1860, Su Shun was supervisor and tried to have his private secretary and staff member, Kao Mou, recommended for first place. But when one of the examiners discovered Kao's paper in the pile dealt out to him he announced to the others in a loud voice: "Listen, all of you! This is Kao Mou's paper. I am determined not to give it full credit. You may do what you like, and even if there is a complaint, I take complete responsibility." Then he marked it with a filled-in circle, the mark for eighty percent. The others all followed his example and gave the paper the identical grade, with the result that Su Shun's hope came to naught, and Kao Mou was passed in the fifteenth place in the second group of candidates.

Because irregularities did take place and the government was concerned to prevent abuses, some high officials were assigned especially to review the papers after the results of the palace examination had been announced. They were not concerned with the quality of the workmanship, of course, but had to look for compliance with the different formal regulations. If they found a defect, even if this happened after the great ceremony and the man had already received his degree from the emperor personally, his place in the order of awards might be shifted, or he might even be placed at the very bottom of the list. It was best to catch this kind of mistake before the names were engraved upon the stele that was to be placed before the temple of Confucius.

THE PALACE EXAMINATION AS A SETTING FOR RETRIBUTION Good or bad luck, as well as the partiality of the readers, played an unavoidable role in determining the results of the palace examination, but there were almost no accounts of supernatural interferences such as were reported for the provincial and metropolitan examinations. Since this examination was held in the palace under the emperor's personal auspices, undoubtedly ghosts were afraid to present themselves. If they were going to appear, most likely they would come to the provincial or metropolitan examinations.

What, then, was the explanation of the role of luck in this examination conducted in the very presence of the emperor? It was not unreasonable to think that it was due to the secret influence of the power of the King of the Dead. Especially since only one man out of ten million had the good fortune to become a first-place *chin-shih*, the successful man was thought to have performed unknown deeds of merit sufficient to deserve so high an honor. The belief was that only the King of the Dead knew about this, secretly pulled the strings, and, through the agency of the emperor and the examination officials, used this brilliant occasion to bestow his rewards upon the meritorious scholar.

In the Ming period a poor graduate of the provincial examination named Lo Lun came all the way from Kiangsi to the capital in order to take the metropolitan examination. When he arrived in Soochow he stayed at an inn where he had been a customer before. That night the great Sung statesman Fan Chung-yen appeared to him in a dream and told him, "I think this time you will probably get your wish and become top man." When, surprised, Lo Lun asked why, the answer came: "You have already forgotten it, but when you stayed at this inn several years ago a young girl tempted you. Your valor in resisting her was very great, and since you turned this valor to your studies, I think this is a proper outcome." Then he left.

Delighted by his good fortune, Lo continued upon his way until he came to Shantung, where, while staying overnight in an inn, his servant, unseen by anyone, found and picked up a gold bracelet in the garden. Without telling anyone, the servant hid the bracelet and took it along. When on the second day after leaving the inn Lo unexpectedly ran short of funds, he confided in the servant, who, with a loyal expression on his face, produced the bracelet and suggested that they sell it and divide the profit. Startled, Graduate Lo scolded the servant and said they should immediately go back and return it. The servant suggested instead that since it looked like they would be late for the examination, they should return the bracelet on their way home. Graduate Lo first thought that there was some point in this plan but then scolded himself for his selfishness and said, "I can take the examination many times, but perhaps a maid of the inn dropped the owner's bracelet accidentally. This may be a serious matter involving a person's life. Your suggestion will not do." And, taking the servant along, he turned back to Shantung.

And indeed, there had been a great commotion at the inn when the gold bracelet disappeared. The proprietor's wife had forgotten that she had placed the bracelet in the basin while she was washing her face, and the maid had thrown it out into the garden along with the water. Believing that the maid was a thief, the lady had her punished physically, while she herself was roundly scolded by her husband as a bad wife. The lady and the maid both proclaimed their innocence, wept until they were dizzy, and were so agitated that they tried to hang themselves. At this point Graduate Lo appeared to return the bracelet, and it became clear what actually had happened. The maid knelt and worshiped him, calling him a living god.

Graduate Lo had lost three or four days and, afraid to be late for the examination, hurried without a moment's delay, day and night, toward Peking. Fortunately he arrived on the day before the beginning of the examination and was able to enter the compound. He passed the metropolitan examination without further ado and when he took the palace examination did indeed come in first, just as Fan Chung-yen had told him he would in his dream. First-place *chinshih* Lo left many writings and was highly honored as a distinguished thinker during the time of the Ming rulers.

In another incident from the Ming period, a provincial examination graduate named Wang Hua stayed in the house of a high minister as a teacher to the family. Although the minister had many concubines, he did not have a single child. One evening the most beautiful of the concubines tried to enter Wang's room, but he, startled, firmly closed the door and did not let her in. Then she said, "I have actually come on the master's order. If you are in doubt, please look at this," and slipped a piece of paper under the door. When Wang looked at it he saw the sentence, "I want an heir," written in the master's hand. Wang wrote underneath, "You startle the gods on high," and returned it. Next year he went to Peking, where he was successful in the metropolitan examination and came in first in the palace examination.

At that time a Taoist was asked into the house of a high official to conduct services for his ancestors, when, in the middle of his duties, he fell into a deep sleep from which he would not awake. When finally he did wake up he said, "Just now the examination took place in heaven. Since I attended it, I was delayed waiting for the gate to open."

"Oh, there are examinations in heaven too? Who came in first?"

"I forget the name, but I remember that there was a procession in front of the man's horse, headed by a banner on which was written,

"You startle the gods on high." This Wang Hua was none other than the father of Wang Yang-ming, the famous thinker of the Ming period.

These are examples of men who, in addition to possessing outstanding mental ability, obtained first place by accumulating virtuous deeds unknown to others. It was also believed that the reverse happened, and that the glory of coming in first would elude a man if he secretly did bad deeds, even if he was the master of many talents.

When, during the Sung dynasty, provincial examination graduate Ting Sheng stayed in the capital for the palace examination, he met a fortuneteller who took a long look at his face and said, "You have a most auspicious appearance and will certainly come in first in this palace examination. If you do not believe this statement, let us write it out," and he wrote "First-Place Chin-shih Ting" on the wall of the inn. A few days later Ting Sheng invited some friends to go gambling with him. Since luck was with him he won six thousand strings of cash in no time at all. While he was still pleased with himself over this stroke of luck, the fortuneteller turned up again and, looking at his face, said, "How strange! Something unexpected has happened. Have you done something wrong? Did I make a mistake? Your appearance now is certainly not that of a first-place *chin-shih*."

Startled, Ting Sheng confessed to the gambling. When he asked the fortuneteller what he should do now, the latter replied, "Meet the friends you defeated and quickly return their money. The first place is out of the question for you, but it looks as if you can still be among those who excel." Ting Sheng quickly called his friends and returned the money. When the palace examination results were announced someone else had taken first place, and he was listed sixth.

In the T'ang period Li Sheng was by far the best in the provincial examination, where he was listed as the top man, but afterward he was successively unlucky and in the end did not obtain the *chin-shih*. Therefore he went to the famous Taoist Yeh for a consultation. Yeh secluded himself in another room for a while, performed some incantations, and finally returned to his seat. Then he said, "Right after the first examination, did you not seduce a virgin in a neighboring house?"

"Now that I think about it, I did try—but without success."

"Failure or success is irrelevant; the deed itself was bad. You were supposed to come in first in the next metropolitan examination but the Heavenly King, knowing of this, demoted you to the twenty-ninth place in the second group as punishment."

"In that case why did I not graduate in the twenty-ninth place in the second group?"

"Wait, there is more. You quarreled with your elder brother over the boundary line between your properties, so the Heavenly King demoted you to the thirty-eighth place in the third group."

"But I did not pass even in that rank."

"Wait, there is still more. While you were staying in the capital you deceived a married woman. This wickedness you consummated. Now you are plotting to seduce other virgins. Therefore, there is no question about your being able to pass. Heaven's punishment will persist for the rest of your life and you will be forced to expiate your crimes."

Li's face turned the color of earth, and all his repentance did not suffice, so that he had to spend the rest of his days in discontent until at last he died.

This tale conjures up a fearful world in which the King of the Dead and the King of Heaven, using their subordinates as antennas extended into the world of the living, catch the good and bad deeds of men and give out appropriate rewards and punishments. A man cannot be careless for a moment. This is the idea at the basis of the Taoist ethic that is commonly practiced in China.

In this way unfairness on the part of the readers was turned into a consequence of the candidate's karma. Each time the examination results were announced some rumor or other circulated: "Oh dear, number so-and-so succeeded on account of a bribe!" "Dear me, number so-and-so is well known for his lack of skill!" "Oh dear, number so-and-so is not a man of good character!" Such criticisms could easily arise, but they were countered with the defense that the first man belonged to a family in which unknown virtue had been accumulated in previous generations, that the second man was a filial son, and that the third had performed good deeds unknown to the world.

Thus a certain licentiate, enraged at having failed the provincial examination, reviled the examiners as being illiterate, when a nearby Taoist commented, "It does not look that way. In general, your essays were simply bad."

This made the *sheng-yüan* all the angrier, and he flared up at the Taoist. "You silly old ass of a Taoist! What essays do you understand!"

The Taoist replied, all the calmer, "To write an essay a tranquil state of mind usually is necessary; it is hardly possible to write a good essay when one is as irascible as you."

After this put-down, the *sheng-yüan* was cornered, gave in, and inquired how, in that case, one could write a good essay. The Taoist answered, "Everything is destiny. If it accords with destiny, a man will pass even if his essay is poor. If it does not accord with destiny, he will fail no matter how good his essay. This destiny is actually created by everyone for himself. Now, accumulate as much merit as possible and afterward quietly await your destiny."

"You speak of accumulating merit, but a poor man like myself does not have the power to accumulate merit, so what can I do?" The Taoist earnestly replied, "No, accumulating merit does not consist only in giving money. It is entirely a matter of one's mental attitude. If you keep a good state of mind, that more than anything else is accumulating merit. And nothing is more harmful to this than getting angry when things do not go your way."

The *sheng-yüan* then reflected deeply and changed his own attitude. As a result, in the next examination he passed low on the list.

Here the Taoist religion went to excessive lengths in accepting reality, leaving no room for dissent and thus making it difficult for ideas of reform to arise. Yet ideas that are realistic through and through do have some merit. The government set up exceptionally stiff punishments for wrongdoing in the examinations, and breaches of trust by officials or delinquencies on the part of candidates were handled with more than ordinary severity. Similarly, the morality of popular Taoism had standards especially applicable to the examinations and demanded exceptional strictness of scholars. Many of those taking the examinations were men of the leisured class, who, having money and time, easily became involved in illicit sexual adventures. Therefore that form of license was most strictly prohibited. Next was the danger that they would use the power of wealth to impose hardships upon the poor. Hoping to encourage the protection of the chastity of women and the relief of the distress of the poor as the supreme ways of acquiring merit, the Taoist religion freely held out the reward of a degree. Taoism implied that men are basically equal, are equally entitled to a peaceful life, and that, simply because there are discrepancies in the distribution of wealth and some men are better off than others, the privileged must not use their power to menace the lives of those beneath them. These can be considered most progressive ideas even today.

The Taoist religion was definitely a faith for the common man. It called the good good and the bad bad, frankly recognizing that what was desired was desirable, and it did not marshal difficult arguments to cover up this basic fact of life. In it lay an exceptionally artless morality, which worked itself deeply into the minds of the masses. Because of this appeal it was accepted not only by the lower classes but also by upper-class intellectuals as well, and greatly influenced their way of looking at the examinations.

THE COURT REVIEW Because the palace examination took place in a small hall and was completed in one day, for a long time the results were criticized as being not very reliable. Naturally there was a tendency for luck to play a part in all examinations, but this was especially true in the palace examination because of the emperor's insistence upon making personal decisions. The metropolitan examination was comparatively trustworthy, since it involved the products of three sessions, so there was an old saying: "The top man in the metropolitan examination is the most talented man in the empire; the top man in the palace examination is the luckiest man in the empire."

Even though its results were a matter of chance, the palace examination influenced the rest of a man's life. From the Ming period on, immediately after the announcement of the results of the palace examination the top man was appointed to be a first-class compiler in the Hanlin Academy (Hanlin *yüan hsiu-chuan*), and the other two men of the first group were made second-class compilers (Hanlin *yüan pien-hsiu*). Although that institution is customarily referred to as the Hanlin Academy, it was really a secretariat immediately under the emperor's supervision that compiled books and drafted decrees. Its staff performed editing and compiling tasks and further served as a source of young officials who could be sent to the provinces as the need arose.

Although results of the metropolitan examination inspired greater confidence than those of the palace examination, the latter could hardly be disregarded in giving the new *chin-shih* their initial assignments. However, from the time of Emperor Yung-cheng on, another test was added in an attempt to correct the absurdity of the palace examination. This "court review," as it was called, in form a repetition of the palace examination, was held on the twenty-eighth day of the fourth month under the responsibility of the Hanlin Academy, since it determined who would be assigned to the academy in addition to the top three men. Because the Hanlin Academy was known as a place for "storing talents," it was the most desirable place in which to begin a career. Normally several hundred candidates for eventual high office were stationed there.

The content of the court review varied but generally involved writing a discussion, an edict, a poem, and a memorial. The candidates did not have to answer all parts but could concentrate on their strong points. In fact, to prevent collusion between examiners and candidates, the latter were forbidden to write a large number of poems on the same topic, since the number of poems could be used to identify their author.

After the results had been used to divide the candidates into three groups, the lists of names were presented to the emperor and made public before the tenth day of the fifth month. Those in the first group were assigned to the Hanlin Academy as "bachelors" (*shu-chi-shih*) and allowed to continue their studies there for three years. The next group became low-ranking officials of the central government, and the men in the final group were given assignments in local administrations. For the bachelors there was a kind of graduation test (*san-kuan k'ao-shih*) conducted three years later in the Pao-ho Pavilion, just before the next palace examination. This test consisted of exercises in poetry (*shih* and *fu*). Those bachelors with the best results remained Hanlin compilers or collators, the men in the second group became central-government officials, while those in the third and lowest group had to await assignment as local officials.

Even in this court review the existence of collusion between examiner and examinee often was pointed out. During the Ch'ien-lung era there was a case in which one man contrived to begin his answer with the two characters used in writing his name, another managed to begin with a character that was part of his given name, and a third used a character that functioned as a phonetic element in his family name. Surely it was not accidental that these candidates finished in first, second, and third place, respectively. Injustice and corruption plagued the system right through to the very last examination.

CHAPTER EIGHT

THE MILITARY EXAMINATION SYSTEM

ACCORDING TO THE PRINCIPLES of Chinese government, the civil component and the military were supposed to be like the two wheels of a chariot: if either was neglected, government would not run smoothly. Examinations, too, were divided into civil and military categories, but the former were so much more important than the latter that the term "examination system" itself referred only to the civil service examinations that have been discussed so far. Neither the government nor the public paid much attention to the military examinations, whose graduates were neglected and disdained, but to leave them entirely out of this account would distort the picture of the examination system, including that of the civil service tests themselves.

The military examination system progressed through the same stages as its civil counterpart. To become a military licentiate, or *wu sheng-yüan,* a man had to pass the district, prefectural, and qualifying military examinations. Then he was entitled to take the provincial military examination, after which came the metropolitan military examination. Those who succeeded in the latter became military graduates (*wu kung-shih*) and could compete in the palace military examination to become military *chin-shih*. The only difference between the two was that the military system lacked the extra reexaminations that had been interpolated in the civilian system.

Young men who hoped to become army officers began with the district military examination, which was conducted by the magistrate and consisted of three sessions. In the first, held on the military drill grounds, the candidates had to shoot three arrows from horseback at a man-shaped target about 1.6 meters (5¼ feet) high. If all three arrows hit home, the man received a perfect score (*shuang-hao*); if two hit the mark, he was graded "good" (*tan-hao*); and if only one reached the target he received a pass (*ho-shih*). Those who did not manage to do even that, or who fell from their horse, were eliminated. The rest went on to the second session.

This was held in the garden of the prefectural office and consisted of a marksmanship test (*pu-she*) and a test of military talent (*chi-yung*). In the first the candidates had to shoot five arrows at a target at fifty paces. Those who made four or five hits were graded "excellent," two or three earned a "good," and one hit a "pass," while anyone who did not hit the target at all was failed. The second part consisted of three tests: drawing a bow (*k'ai-kung*), brandishing a sword (*wu-tao*), and weight lifting (*to-shih*). In the first of these the men had to bend a bow into the shape of a full moon, with the bows graded by strength into 120-, 100-, and 80-catty weapons (a catty, or *chin*, weighs approximately 600 grams, or about 21 ounces). A man who bent the heaviest bow received an "excellent," the 100-catty bow earned a "good," and the 80-catty bow gave him a grade of "passing." The next test involved grasping a halberd, *ch'ing-lung tao,* or "green dragon sword," brandishing it in front of one's face, swinging it around one's back and returning it to the front, and finally spinning it like a water wheel, all without once touching it to the ground. Grades were assigned according to the weight of the halberd; men who used the 120-, 100-, or 80-catty weapons were rated "excellent," "good," and "passing," respectively. In the weight-lifting test the candidates were required to raise a stone at least one Chinese foot, or 14 inches, off the ground. Those lifting the heaviest, 300-catty stone received the grade of "excellent." Raising the 250-catty stone earned a man a "good," while lifting a 200-catty stone merited a "pass." These two outdoor tests determined whether a man would pass, but he still had to go through the third session, consisting of an indoor test.

This was a test of scholarship, requiring the candidates to write out several hundred characters from a designated place in the military classics that they were supposed to have memorized. There were seven military classics, but only three of these were used in the examination, the *Sun Tzu, Wu Tzu,* and *Ssu-ma Fa.* Since, however, scholarship was the weak point in men devoted to the military arts, they used all their ingenuity to smuggle miniature books into the examination hall, and the examiners, knowing that the outdoor tests were decisive, closed an eye to this infraction of the rules. If a man was able surreptitiously to copy out the whole passage from the book satisfactorily, he was still doing rather well. Even so, sometimes the candidates made really laughable mistakes in copying. For instance, the two characters 一旦 (*i-tan,* "once"), if written vertically, might be run together to form the character 亘 (*hsüan,* "to revolve"); conversely, the single character 丕 (*p'i,* "great" or "distinguished") might be miscopied as the two characters 不一 (*pu i,* "not one"). Such errors can occur only when someone copies a text without making any effort to understand it. But because the offenders were merely semisavage military men, this deficiency, too, was overlooked.

The men who passed the district military examination were eligible to take the subsequent prefectural military examination, which was just like the first test except that the standards of grading were a little higher.

The men who passed this examination were entitled in turn to take the qualifying military examination administered by the provincial director of studies at the time that he gave the annual examination for scholars. Again the contents of the examination were the same, but this time the number of men to be graduated was limited, so that only those with the best scores were selected for the vacancies. They were assigned to the district military schools as military licentiates, *wu sheng-yüan* or *wu sheng*. Their subsequent careers were parallel with those of their civilian counterparts, and they too had to sit for an "annual" examination at least once in nine years. Many of them went on to the next step and took the provincial military examination.

This was given in the provincial capital early in the tenth month in the same years as the provincial examination for prospective bureaucrats. In charge was the governor general or the governor, and since these were civilians, it was customary for the provincial commander in chief (*t'i-tu*) or brigade general (*tsung-ping*) to attend as an associate examiner. During this examination, in addition to tests of ability in archery while mounted and on foot, the men were examined in bending the bow, brandishing the halberd, and weight lifting. Furthermore, the candidates, while on horseback, had to try to shoot down a round ball from a high place. Inasmuch as it would not drop unless hit in the center, this was a good test of marksmanship. Actually, however, no one ever failed on account of this test because his performance in the other parts of the examination was considered to be more important.

Finally, the candidates had to write out a passage from the military classics. Here, too, this trial did not determine whether a man would pass, although it did influence his standing. Since the number of candidates to be passed was restricted by a quota, it is difficult to generalize, but usually a passing score depended upon achieving five hits from horseback and more than five while standing in the archery tests, and bending the 120-catty bow, brandishing the 120-catty halberd, and lifting the 300-catty stone. Those who qualified received the degree of military graduate, *wu chü-jen*, and could become junior officers. Many of these graduates proceeded to take the metropolitan military examination given in Peking in the same years as its civilian counterpart, but during the ninth month rather than the third.

The first session, lasting from the fifth to the seventh day of the ninth month, consisted of a test in mounted archery given to one man at a time. During those three days the candidates were not shut up in a compound, as were the men who took the metropolitan civil service examination. During the next three days, the eighth through the tenth, the tests in archery on foot and in military skills were administered. These trials determined in general who would pass, and on the eleventh day the results were announced. Generally, out of every hundred men who had earned excellent and good scores, twenty-two were selected to be passed and to participate in the next session. Held on the fourteenth day in the Peking Examination Compound, this began with a bow-bending test to verify past performance and then required the candidates to write out a selection from the military classics. Once again, this written test did not determine whether a man passed but was averaged with his grades from other tests to obtain his overall score. The number of men to be passed was not preset but generally amounted to about a hundred. The recommendations of the examiners were presented to the emperor for his approval.

The palace military examination took place on the last day of the ninth month. First the candidates, assembled in the T'ai-ho Pavilion in the palace, had to write out a selection from the military classics. Then, on the third day of the tenth month, the second session was held in the Tzu-kuang Pavilion in the beautiful West Park (*hsi-yüan*) of the imperial residence, which had served since Ming times as a palace drill ground. The Tzu-kuang Pavilion could be called a military museum also, since in it were displayed war pictures and booty collected by Ch'ing generals while pacifying Sinkiang and in other campaigns. It was customary for the emperor himself to go to the Tzu-kuang Pavilion during the examination and observe the military exercises going on below. There were tests of archery on horseback and on foot. This was not a tournament in the imperial presence, in which one man tried to defeat another. Each man shot three arrows from horseback and two while on foot. Even if he missed the target he was not failed. The remaining tests of martial skill were scheduled for the next day, when bow bending, halberd brandishing, and weight lifting were performed as the emperor watched. Even if the results did not match those attained in the metropolitan military examination, the men were not failed, but they did have to repeat the examination three years later.

Later that same day the examiners ranked the men according to their overall performances and submitted their recommendations to the emperor. After approving them the emperor conducted a degree-granting ceremony on the following day. This ceremony was exactly like that held for the civilian *chin-shih*: again the men were arranged in three groups; and slightly different degrees—*wu chin-shih chi-ti, wu chin-shih ch'u-sheng,* and *t'ung wu chin-shih ch'u-sheng*—were granted to the members in each group, corresponding to those given to civilians.

The new military *chin-shih* received assignments according to the ranking they had won in this palace examination, but were highly regarded neither by the world at large nor in the army itself, because war differs from government, and skill in taking examinations is not necessarily useful on the battlefield. Although civilian *chin-shih,* too, suffered some criticism, many famous statesmen and scholars did issue from their midst, but almost no military *chin-shih* achieved military distinction. The influential leaders in the army were generals who had worked themselves up from the ranks and had shown their mettle in actual combat. The army was a special kind of society of its own, and men who had not experienced from the outset the hardships of military life were unable to handle the common soldiers. No commander can carry out bold tactics without having gained the confidence of his troops, and in emergencies generals who had risen from the ranks were the most reliable. The best fate for a military *chin-shih* was to be stationed in a quiet place and to spend his allotted years there in peace. No wonder society did not value them highly.

CHAPTER NINE

THE SPECIAL EXAMINATIONS

THE EXAMINATION SYSTEM consisted of a sequence of tests in an ascending order of importance, with the standards becoming progressively higher as a candidate advanced through the series. Since the scope of the questions as well as the process of selection were firmly set, there was the danger that at times men of exceptional talents might be overlooked. Moreover, frequently such exceptionally gifted men despised the examinations and even shunned them. Having long before recognized this as the weak point in the established system, the government sometimes conducted special examinations to attract the great talents who had not risen by the usual route. Accordingly, they organized a set of special examinations, *chih-k'o*, analogous to those of the regular system. These special examinations were held by imperial decree at irregular intervals.

Special examinations of this sort were already being used at the beginning of the examination system in the Sui period, and also were employed occasionally during T'ang and Sung times. Although all were called "special examinations," they differed in their purposes, as is indicated by their more specific designations. For example, when, in order to counteract a disagreeable public attitude marked by excessive office-seeking, the government wished to attract and reward well-known private scholars who were living in seclusion and uninterested in careers, it held a special "examination for men living far away in seclusion" (*kao-tao yu-yin k'o*), or an "examination for those hiding in the mountains and forests" (*shan-lin yin-i k'o*). Then the emperor ordered officials to recommend men who were living like hermits in the mountains and forests to come to the palace for a simple examination, thereby holding them up as models for the whole country. But it would be strange for a real thinker living in seclusion to come forth when called by the emperor, since a genuine recluse would decline even an imperial order without a second thought.

Critics sneered that "men come on horseback to attend the examination for those hiding in the mountains and forests," thus satirizing the examination for attracting only men who were just waiting for such an invitation.

The "examination for those hiding in the mountains and forests" may have been rather odd, but not so was the "examination for great scholars of extensive learning," *po-hsüeh hung-tzu,* held in the early Ch'ing period. At the time there was no dearth of Chinese who retained their enmity for the dynasty established by the alien Manchus. But there were also men who, born and raised under the Ming, had advanced to a certain point in their studies only to be deprived of the opportunity to take the examinations during the warfare at the end of the dynasty. When peace was restored they felt that it would be foolish for them to rub shoulders with younger men in competitive examinations. Quite a few old scholars who had no special antipathy toward the Ch'ing rulers continued their studies in private, since they had missed the chance to take the examinations. But for the Ch'ing to obtain the support of these neutral old scholars by drawing them into the government was a matter of major import for their control over China. Thus in 1678, thirty-four years after the Ch'ing dynasty had been established in Peking, the emperor K'ang-hsi conducted the first "examination for great scholars" and ordered central and local officials to suggest such eminent men. Recommendations of scholars already in office were acceptable, of course, but the object was to bring forth old men left over from the Ming dynasty. If only one such distinguished scholar appeared, the government would score a great propaganda success.

Although at that time the dynasty faced the rebellion of Wu San-kuei in the south, a continuous stream of old scholars flowed into Peking in compliance with the emperor's decree. Despite the war-time confusion, their number reached 143. On the third day of the first month of 1679, Emperor K'ang-hsi ordered the Board of Rites and the Hanlin Academy to prepare the examination, gave a banquet in the T'i-jen Pavilion, and tested the assembled scholars on their knowledge of poetry and rhymed prose. He selected twenty to graduate in the top group, placed another thirty in a second group, and assigned all fifty to various offices within the Hanlin Academy charged with compiling the history of the Ming dynasty.

Representative of those who were awarded degrees at that time is Chu I-tsun, far better known by his pen name Chu-chih. It has always been difficult for most men to combine scholarship and literary ability, yet Chu-chih not only displayed a deep knowledge of the classics in many of his works but also was distinguished as a writer and poet. Born under the last of the Ming emperors, he was only sixteen years old when the dynasty fell and thus belonged to the war genera-tion. Being poor, and living as he did in a time of uninterrupted warfare, he missed the examinations. At the age of fifty, then, he could accept without a guilty conscience that special invitation from the victorious dynasty.

But the situation was different for slightly older men. Aside from those who had already submitted to the Ch'ing and become licentiates or officials, those who were living aloof from the conquerors as simple commoners were perplexed. Should they refuse the invitation, and continue for the rest of their lives to remain in the country as men of the Ming, yet in compensation win lasting fame for their refusal to serve the foreign dynasty? Or should they, in light of the political situation, accept the invitation, gain their proper place in society, take advantage of their studies, and acquire status also for their descendants? Wang Fu-shih, ten years Chu Chu-chih's senior, and still older men, such as Ku Yen-wu and Huang Tsung-hsi, were already more than sixty years of age and from the very start had opposed the Ch'ing. Thus, even if recommended they would have refused. Such a stubborn one was a seventy-year-old scholar by the name of Fu Shan. He was forcefully recommended by a local official, and his repeated refusals of the honor were not accepted. Since he had no other recourse, he hitched his donkey to a cart and, with his son driving, went as far as the outskirts of Peking. Once there he took refuge in a dilapidated temple and, pleading illness, would go no farther. High court ministers, hearing about this, tried to induce him to come to the palace, but Fu Shan persisted in maintaining that he was sick, until finally the emperor allowed him to return to his village.

After the examination some people said that the examiners had been illiterate and the results were unfair. Such criticism left a bad impression, so Emperor K'ang-hsi ordered that a certain number of men with respectable scores who had been passed over in the selection should be chosen for appointment to office. Among these was an old scholar named Sun Chih-wei. When the officials from the Board of Personnel who were administering the examination saw Sun's snow-white hair they said that he was a bit too old. Offended, Sun replied: "From the start I declined to take part in this examination because I was too old, but at that time an official, saying I was still young, forced me on. And now I say again that, because I am too old, I would not embark on an official career for anything. And you too say I am too old. That is exactly the way it is!" After their outburst of laughter the officials granted Sun's request that he be allowed to return to his native village. This sort of conduct seems to be characteristic of officials, wherever they may be.

The Emperor K'ang-hsi's successor, Yung-cheng, also ordered an "examination for great scholars" late in his reign. This actually was held under his successor, Ch'ien-lung. At that time, out of 176 candidates, only 5 received degrees in the first group and 10 in the second. This reduction in the scope of rewards of the special examination was the result of a secret feud between special and regular degree-holders. To the latter, who had obtained their *chin-shih* the hard way, it was mortifying that those who passed the special examinations would receive immediately, after just that one test, greater honors than they themselves would be accorded. Actually, during the reign of K'ang-hsi the special degree-holders assigned to the Hanlin Academy were treated by the regular degree-holders already entrenched there much like a new bride is treated by her sisters-in-law in an extended Chinese household. Indeed, they were given such a hard time that, gossips said, Chu Chu-chih alone remained to uphold the honor of the special degree-holders. Since the examiners were officials of the Hanlin Academy, they marked the answer papers so strictly that, as we have seen, very few men passed the examination under Emperor Ch'ien-lung.

After the Ch'ien-lung era the special examinations were allowed to lapse and the regular examination system was left without competition. In time the memory of the special examinations became dim, and among men who failed to obtain a degree there was talk of "the good old days," when culture flourished, and scholars were well treated, and the special system permitted talented men to congregate at court. The number of those wrapped in their dreams and singing the praises of the K'ang-hsi and Ch'ien-lung eras increased until they influenced the court to consider reviving the special examinations. Ultimately, however, because of strong pressure from regular degree-holders, the idea was dropped.

CHAPTER TEN

AN EVALUATION OF THE EXAMINATION SYSTEM

DID THE EXAMINATION SYSTEM SERVE A USEFUL PURPOSE? The examination system, with its long series of tests, involved considerable expense for the government, while for the candidates the cost was more psychological and physical than financial. Such sacrifices called for commensurate returns. Leaving aside for the moment the individuals involved in the system, let us consider what benefits Chinese society derived from it. In order to do this judiciously, we must consider the system not just as it operated in one period, but rather in terms of its long history.

The purpose of instituting the examinations, some fourteen hundred years ago under the Sui rulers, was to strike a blow against government by the hereditary aristocracy, which had prevailed until then, and to establish in its place an imperial autocracy. The period of disunion lasting from the third to the sixth century was the golden age of the Chinese aristocracy: during that time it controlled political offices in central and local governments. In certain ways, this rule by aristocrats was similar to that of the Fujiwara family in Heian-period Japan (794–1185), and in other ways to that of clan rulers in feudal Japan. But there were also differences: in Japan the Fujiwara family alone was supreme, whereas in China a considerable number of aristocratic families, divided roughly into four groups, dominated the country. Another difference between the Chinese system and that which prevailed in feudal Japan was the fact that in China the first son did not automatically inherit his father's status, as he did in Japan. In China a son's initial status and the limits to which he could rise were determined by his ancestry.

The important point in China, as in Japan, was that the power of the aristocracy seriously constrained the emperor's power to appoint officials. He could not employ men simply on the basis of their ability, since any imperial initiative to depart from the traditional personnel policy evoked a sharp counterattack from the aristocratic officials. This was the situation when the Sui emperor, exploiting the fact that he had reestablished order and that his authority was at its height, ended the power of the aristocracy to become officials merely by virtue of family status. He achieved this revolution when he enacted the examination system (and provided that only its graduates were to be considered qualified to hold government office), kept at hand a reserve of such officials, and made it a rule to use only them to fill vacancies in central and local government as they occurred. This was the origin of the examination system.

The Sui dynasty was soon replaced by the T'ang, which for the most part continued the policies of its predecessor. Actually, as the T'ang was in the process of winning control over China, a new group of aristocrats appeared who hoped to transmit their privileges to their descendants. To deal with this problem the emperor used the examination system and favored its *chin-shih,* trying to place them in important posts so that he could run the government as he wished. The consequence was strife between the aristocrats and the *chin-shih,* with the contest gradually turning in favor of the latter. Since those who gained office simply through their parentage were not highly regarded, either by the imperial government or by society at large, career-minded aristocrats, too, seem to have found it necessary to enter officialdom through the examination system. Their acceptance of this hard fact meant a real defeat for the aristocracy.

Of the thirty-one men who served as chief minister during the reign of the mid-T'ang emperor Hsüan-tsung (713–56), eleven, or about one-third, were *chin-shih.* About a hundred years later, however, during the reign of Emperor Hsien-tsung (806–21), the representation was just about reversed: of twenty-five chief ministers, fifteen, or about three-fifths, were *chin-shih.* Under these circumstances, the aristocracy did not sit idly by. Families that were able to adapt early to the change in policy were able to remain eminent for a long time. Thus, the aristocratic Lu family of Fan-yang responded to the changing times by exerting themselves in the examination system, shaping every opportunity to their advantage. As a result, by the end of the dynasty they had produced 116 *chin-shih.* Other families, too, were able to accomplish comparable successes precisely because they were aristocrats.

But those families who, unlike the Lu, continued to boast of their aristocratic ancestry and made light of the examinations as something plebeian and beneath them, came to regret their folly. The eminent aristocrat Hsüeh Yüan-ch'ao, reminiscing in old age, told of the three great mistakes in his life: the first was not taking the examinations and becoming a *chin-shih;* the second was his marriage to a girl from a family of low status; and the third was his failure to become the cultural director at court. The first of those errors was by far the most serious.

Actually, the sons of high ministers and great generals, by virtue of their fathers' status, had a right to hold minor offices without going through the examinations. When the sons of aristocrats pushed their way into the examinations intended for the sons of members of the lower class, who had no powerful connections, they were behaving much like wealthy students of today who encroach upon the opportunities offered their poorer fellows by vying for part-time jobs. This opposition between aggressive aristocrats and resentful commoners persisted until the Sung period. But this did not stop men of both groups from taking the examination route to success. By the time of the T'ang dynasty, general opinion held that it was good for both aristocrats and commoners to take the examinations on the same level, stressing the equal opportunities offered them because of the impartiality of the examination system.

This trend was most welcome to the emperors. At the beginning of the T'ang period, the emperors, seeking an alternative to government by aristocrats, had used the civil bureaucracy as a net by which gradually to pull in officials from among the commoners. At last, as a result of their perseverance, they were actually catching the aristocrats themselves. The man who first conceived the idea of spreading the net was Emperor T'ai-tsung (r. 627–50). After an examination, while observing the splendid sight of the new *chin-shih* leaving the government building in a triumphant column, T'ai-tsung exclaimed, "The heroes of the empire are all in my pocket!" Actually, however, it took the entire three hundred years of the T'ang dynasty for the emperors to get those conceited high aristocrats into their pockets.

The T'ang can be regarded as a period of transition from the aristocratic government inherited from the time of the Six Dynasties to the purely bureaucratic government of future regimes. The examination system made a large contribution to what was certainly a great advance for China's society, and in this respect its immense significance in Chinese history cannot be denied. Furthermore, that change was begun fourteen hundred years ago, at about the time when in Europe the feudal system had scarcely been formed. In comparison, the examination system was immeasurably progressive, containing as it did a superb idea the equal of which could not be found anywhere else in the world at that time.

This is not to say that the T'ang examination system was without defects. First, the number of those who passed through it was extremely small. In part this was an inevitable result of the limited diffusion of China's literary culture at a time when printing had not yet become practical and hand-copied books were still both rare and expensive, thus restricting the number of men able to pursue scholarly studies. Furthermore, because the historical and economic roots of the new bureaucratic system were still shallow, matters did not always go smoothly and sometimes there were harsh factional conflicts among officials. The development of those conflicts indicates that they were caused by the examination system itself and constituted a second serious defect.

As has been indicated, a master-disciple relationship between the examiner and the men he passed was established, much like that between a political leader and his henchmen, while the men who passed the examination in the same year considered one another as classmates and helped one another forever after. When such combinations became too strong, factions were born. Since at that time an examiner could gain a large following almost without effort, the position of examiner itself became an object of contention, and innumerable small cliques were formed centering on the selection of examiners. But when they were challenged by men whose power lay outside the examination system, the *chin-shih* would join in one great group to combat them, in contests that sometimes swayed back and forth for as long as forty years. When the *chin-shih* controlled the empire, all officials who were not *chin-shih* were removed from the central government; and when the latter won control, they in turn sent all the *chin-shih* into the provinces. Since this sort of ebb and flow occurred over and over again, there were repeated abrupt reversals of governmental domestic and foreign policy, with the result that in the end the authority of the central government itself was damaged. Thus, Emperor Wen-tsung (r. 827–41) was moved to complain that to defeat foreign bandits was simple but that to prevent cliques at court was impossible.

These two defects of the examination system were eliminated during the Sung regime. For one thing, the number of men who were granted degrees suddenly rose, indicating a similar rise in the number of candidates. This was made possible by the increase in productive power and the consequent accumulation of wealth, which was the underlying reason that Chinese society changed so greatly from the T'ang period to the Sung. A new class appeared in China, comparable to the bourgeoisie in early modern Europe. In China this newly risen class concentrated hard on scholarship, and with the custom of this group, publishers prospered mightily. The classic books of Buddhism and Confucianism were printed; the collected writings of contemporaries and their discourses and essays on current topics were published; and the government issued an official gazette, so that in a sense China entered upon an age of mass communications. As a result learning was so widespread that candidates for the examinations came from virtually every part of the land, and the government could freely pick the best among them to form a reserve of officials.

In the Sung dynasty the system of conducting the examinations every three years was established. Since about three hundred men were selected each time, the government obtained an average of one hundred men a year who were qualified for the highest government positions. Thus the most important positions in government were occupied by *chin-shih,* and no longer were there conflicts between men who differed in their preparatory backgrounds, such as those between *chin-shih* and non–*chin-shih* that had arisen in the T'ang period.

Another improvement made during the Sung period was the establishment of the palace examination as the apex of the normal examination sequence. Under the T'ang emperors the conduct of the examinations was completely entrusted to officials, but this does not mean that emperors neglected them, because they were held by imperial order. It even happened that Empress Wu (r. 684–705) herself conducted the examinations in an attempt to win popularity, but according to public opinion of the time she was meddling in the business of officials and the response to her act was overwhelmingly adverse. The real problem in letting officials conduct the examinations was that the formation of links between examiners and successful candidates could easily damage the fairness of the system. Therefore, Emperor T'ai-tsu instituted the palace examination to follow the metropolitan examination. He decreed that the examiners and the candidates they passed should not call each other master and disciple; that the emperor was the master of all *chin-shih;* that they were his disciples; that the master-disciple relationship was to be established between himself and them; and that officials who became political leaders with a personal following would be guilty of infringing upon imperial authority. In other words, the emperor himself now became the leader of a political party composed of *chin-shih.* The old practice and the factionalism it entailed did not disappear completely, of course, but now those factions were much more limited in extent and a strong-minded emperor could disregard them. They came to have little influence in organizing men.

The position of the emperor in the political system changed greatly from T'ang times to Sung. No longer did the emperor consult on matters of high state policy with two or three great ministers deep in the interior of the palace, far removed from actual administrators. Now he was an autocrat, directly supervising all important departments of government and giving instructions about every aspect of government. Even minor matters of personnel needed imperial sanction. Now the emperor resembled the pivot of a fan, without which the various ribs of government would fall apart and be scattered. The creation of the palace examination as the final examination, given directly under the emperor's personal supervision, went hand in hand with this change in his function in the nation's political machinery and was a necessary step in the strengthening of imperial autocracy.

Thus, the examination system changed, along with Chinese society as a whole. Created to meet an essential need, it changed in response to that society's demand. It was most effective in those early stages when, first in the T'ang period, it was used by the emperor to suppress the power of the aristocracy, and then later, in the Sung period, when the cooperation of young officials with the *chin-shih* was essential for the establishment of imperial autocracy. Therefore, in the early Sung years *chin-shih* enjoyed very rapid promotion; this was especially true of the first-place *chin-shih*, not a few of whom rose to the position of chief councilor in fewer than ten years.

However, the vicissitudes of institutions in the history of a nation do not differ much from those in a man's life. At the beginning there were many vacancies in government offices, and *chin-shih* were scarce. Therefore, the examination system flourished and *chin-shih* were selected. But as the process was continued, the number of *chin-shih* became excessive, while the number of suitable openings declined. Since the government did not reduce the number of *chin-shih* being produced, even when it was already too late to do so, and the rate of granting degrees continued unabated, it became difficult to find posts for graduates, so that the examination system ended by being a burden on the government.

Therefore, successive regimes had to keep reappraising the examination system. This assessment began during the reign of Emperor Shen-tsung (r. 1068–86), in the middle of the Northern Sung period, when Wang An-shih was the chief minister. Convinced that reliance upon the examinations alone was unsatisfactory, Wang believed that it was necessary to foster outstanding talents and that for this a fresh start in education was necessary. Therefore, he founded new schools, a most progressive idea for the time. In the capital a first-rate national university was established and equipped with eighty dormitories, each housing thirty students. It was a truly admirable institution that provided instruction to twenty-four hundred students at a time.

After the collapse of the Northern Sung dynasty, the school system was continued almost as before by the Southern Sung, and its graduates could enter government service with the same standing as graduates of the examination system. Wang An-shih's view seems to have been that someday the examination system would be abolished and officials would be selected solely from among the university graduates. Although this goal would not be realized, the fact that the school system operated alongside the examination system indicates the progressive nature of Sung society.

Unfortunately, the educational system that had been set up with such care was unable completely to supplant the examination system, probably for economic reasons. Education always costs money. And governments everywhere are apt to economize on such programs as education, which do not show immediate gains. At the beginning of the Southern Sung period the size of the national university was reduced from what it had been under the Northern Sung.

Afterward, reversing the course of progress, there was a decline in public schooling in China. During the Ming and Ch'ing dynasties a national university was maintained in the capital, as were prefectural and district schools in the provinces, but those were schools in name only and they did not actually offer instruction. On the contrary, the school system was absorbed by the examination system, so that what originally had been school examinations became merely examinations preparatory to those of the examination system itself. Therefore we can really say that the school system disappeared and only the examination system survived. The latter was not inexpensive, but it was cheap compared with the cost of maintaining a school system. An exceptionally easygoing government ruined the fine school system that had been created during the Northern Sung period.

Yet in the Ming and Ch'ing regimes, too, the examination system in its own way showed some positive results, at least at the beginning of those dynasties. The Ming was Chinese, while the Ch'ing was foreign, but they were alike in that they had been founded by military force. Once they had gained control over the land, they could not rule by military strength alone but needed the cooperation of powerful civil bureaucrats. During these critical periods it was mandatory for the rulers to obtain talented officials, and through the examination system, disregarding matters of mere form, they were able to choose really capable men. As a result, some outstanding statesmen were found among those *chin-shih* who had excelled in the examinations.

During the long duration of the Ch'ing dynasty, the best years of the examination system were those prior to the Ch'ien-lung era. Later there was a surplus of potential officials and the examinations were conducted simply for the sake of complying with earlier precedents. Now those "students" who took the examinations were merely office-seekers, crowding around the compounds like ants converging on sugar. Generally, because of the long period of peace, the candidates had made some progress in scholarship, and their papers were often so similar in quality that the examiners found it difficult to make their selections. Under such circumstances, the officials who administered the examinations had to think more about how to eliminate candidates than about how to select the best scholars, and they devised various complicated formal requirements that in the end destroyed the true purpose of the whole system.

The situation was especially bad in the late Ch'ing period because, in addition to the fact that the system itself was out of date, officials were improvising merely technical reforms to check the deteriorating discipline within the bureaucracy. Therefore, it is not fair to appraise the system in terms of one period alone. When we see it in the perspective of its long history, we must conclude that there was a time when it contributed much that was of value to Chinese society.

IDEAL AND REALITY IN THE EXAMINATION SYSTEM   For a long time the examination system has been criticized from different points of view and found to be seriously defective, but the fact that it lasted for more than thirteen hundred years shows that it also had its strong points. Let us now consider some of its outstanding ideals.

First, in principle it was open to all qualified applicants. It is true that some men were barred from qualifying because they themselves, or their fathers or grandfathers, had engaged in a "base occupation." But those were exceptional cases, for which Chinese society had its own rationale. With those few exceptions, the examination system was unusually democratic, being open to anyone, regardless of his social background.

This is not to say that in fact everyone was equally able to take advantage of it, for always the economic problem was present. Since the examination route was long and the competition intense, men who achieved the glory of a *chin-shih* degree in their twenties were most fortunate. Those who did so in their thirties were by no means behind schedule. But for a man to continue his studies without interruption for such a long period required a degree of economic support that was simply not available to poor people. Furthermore, although no examination fees were charged, taking the examinations was nevertheless a very expensive process. Aside from the travel and lodging expenses incurred during a trip to the provincial capital, everyone had to pay for thank-you gifts for the examiners and tips for the staff, and could not avoid sharing the costs of banquets and other kinds of entertainment. The expenses of those who went on to take the metropolitan and palace examinations became very high indeed. During the late Ming period, in the sixteenth century, it is said that these costs came to around six hundred ounces of silver. Converted into modern currency on the basis of the amount of rice that money would have bought, this sum today would enable a couple to take a trip around the world in comfort.

Thus, although there were no examination fees, a poor man, even if he had some travel funds, could not attain what for him was an inaccessible peak. However, such inequity is hardly peculiar to the Chinese examination system. Perfect justice is impossible at all times by the very nature of the world; and even today, when the principle of equality in educational opportunity is accepted, there is no country in the world where everyone actually receives the same education. In our opinion today, participation in the Chinese examination system was too expensive for the candidate, when the whole burden of obtaining an education rested on the individual and his family, while the government did not concern itself about operating a school system to offer education for everyone. Yet, from a different perspective, we can observe that the people's wealth was increasing and that, as has been noted, from the Sung period on there was a dramatic increase in the productivity of the Chinese economy and an attendant rise in the wealth and numbers of the middle class. The examination system actually dealt with this class, which had the surplus resources to meet the expenses of education and of the many different examinations.

Seen in this light, the contention that the doors of the examination system were open to all applicants was an exaggeration, of course. But here, too, we must not lose sight of the historical context: the very idea that everyone should be eligible for the examinations, regardless of family background or lineage, was incomparably forward-looking in its day. Nonetheless, from Sung times until very recently, the Chinese social structure changed very little, and the discrepancies between the rich and the poor continued to be extreme. During that long interval the examination system, too, continued with minimum change. Compared with European institutions, it was extremely progressive at its beginning—and very far behind the times at its end.

A second strong point of the system, again in theory, was its fairness. Thus, examiners saw only the seat number on an answer paper and did not know who wrote it; and in the prefectural and metropolitan examinations they did not see the original answer at all but only a copy, a precaution unique even today. The faith people had in the examinations, and the honor they showed to those scholars who succeeded in them, attest the general trust in the system's fairness.

But this also had its limits; all too often fairness was compromised by corrupt candidates and examiners. When the competition became too stiff, some candidates felt that they must pass at any cost and, in the end, turned to dishonest methods. Once such a dishonest act succeeded, other candidates felt that they would be hurt unless they acted in the same way, so gradually the evil spread. They brought miniature books to the examinations, or wrote classical texts over an entire undergarment. Still worse was the hiring of substitutes to take the examinations. Some substitutes were so well paid that they easily set themselves up in business. Experts appeared who would contract their services to any number of men. This corruption was especially bad in the late Ch'ing period, toward the end of the nineteenth century, when an agency that prospered first during the Nanking provincial examinations became known throughout the country. The abuses finally affected Peking, too: when a man named Liu wrote two papers in addition to his own in the metropolitan examination, not only did all the papers pass, but one came in first. The scandalous tale finally reached the ears of the palace examination readers, who took care not to give him a high ranking and ended by placing all three papers in the third group. Instead of receiving an assignment in the Hanlin Academy, Liu (who wrote a beautiful hand) was given a trivial post. This was his punishment for having made so much money.

The candidates themselves not only did dishonest things but also, to be safe, involved the examiners as well in their schemes. It was a weak point of the Chinese bureaucratic system that, moved by a sense of obligation that made them unable to refuse repeated requests, men who had been appointed examiners would be involved before they knew it in collusion (*kuan-chieh*), and thereby become parties to an illegal undertaking.

Public opinion, however, was most sensitive to this kind of injustice. The public examined the lists with a sharp eye, and if the names of too many sons of high government officials or of too many friends of the examiners appeared on them, public opinion was immediately agitated. In China this counted for a good deal. When an injustice was too great, public opinion could deliver a blow so severe that a man would never recover from it. For example, in 1699 the provincial examination in Peking, conducted by an old chief examiner called Chiang Ch'en-ying and associate examiner Li P'an-tung, was criticized for flagrant bribery. Indeed, among those who passed were many sons of high government officials, including four or five cabinet ministers and several dozen ministers of state. Moreover, those favored sons finished high on the list. This evidence of collusion led to rumblings of public opinion and the appearance of street posters charging favoritism. Finally Emperor K'ang-hsi heard of it, arrested the examiners, and launched an inquiry. Chief Examiner Chiang Ch'en-ying, who had become a *chin-shih* only two years earlier although he was already more than seventy years old at the time, was too frail a man to endure prison life and soon died of malnutrition.

As a result, the facts of the case remained obscure to the end, but the charges on the posters, to the effect that three thousand ounces of silver had been paid by so-and-so and ten thousand ounces by so-and-so, probably were not entirely fabricated. In any event, the associate examiner was sentenced to banishment to the frontier.

After such an incident the system would function honestly for a while, but ten years or so later things were apt to revert to their normal corrupt state. To deal with this continuing problem the government added a variety of reexaminations, thereby certainly increasing the misery of the candidates. Other than that there was nothing the government could do but exert itself to achieve fairness. To the very end the government, or at least the emperor, wanted to maintain the integrity of the examinations. They were criticized in a society for which they provided the major topic of conversation, and people clung to the frail hope provided by their faith in the emperor's fair-mindedness.

THE MISERIES AND REVOLTS OF THOSE WHO FAILED   To become an official was the most lucrative as well as the most honorable career in imperial China. Therefore the sons of the propertied intelligentsia converged upon the narrow gates of the examination system, doing their best to pass through them. Those who succeeded all the way to the *chin-shih* degree were delighted, naturally, but inevitably the system also produced a large number of men who experienced the bitterness of repeated failure and spent gloomy lives in hopeless despondency, lamenting their misfortune.

In the T'ang period, when learning had not yet been widely diffused, the number of candidates was not as large as it was to become later, and yet even then, in the final examination for the *chin-shih* only one or two candidates out of a hundred passed. With the Sung period the number of candidates increased dramatically. Six or seven thousand men traveled from the provinces to the capital for the metropolitan examination, and double that number actually turned up to take the tests. Usually not more than three hundred were graduated, a ratio of about one success in fifty hopeful candidates.

During the Ming and Ch'ing dynasties the competition became worse with the passage of time. The difficulty of becoming a licentiate varied from region to region, but the highest barrier was the provincial examination, for only one out of a hundred licentiates succeeded in becoming a graduate. In the following metropolitan examination one out of thirty candidates was passed, but that involved the toughest competition among the best candidates in the nation. Counting only those licentiates throughout the country who actually took the examinations, about one man out of every three thousand licentiates had the great good fortune to receive the *chin-shih* degree.

Those who concentrated upon scholarship were, of course, men of a certain means. In addition it was possible for licentiates and graduates, enjoying a status high above that of ordinary men, to seek a secondary occupation. Yet there were also enthusiasts who, managing very poorly, devoted themselves to their studies, making a last stand in tragic awareness of their plight and defying the examinations to do their worst. The hard blows they suffered are indescribable. To quote a T'ang poet:

> Failure after failure:
> Painful as a sword wound . . .

Continuing the poem, he lamented that when he went out-of-doors the grass and trees rustling in the wind and the clouds floating in the sky reminded him of his grief; and that when he returned to his lodgings and went to bed, he slept lightly, waking up nine times during the night, never seeing his native village even in his dreams, for they were short and the way home was long.

Some men, although discouraged, did not abandon hope and planned to turn failure into success, while others, conscious of their helplessness, resigned themselves to fate. But talented and actively ambitious men who experienced the bitterness of repeated failure often went from disappointment to desperation, and from desperation to revolt. Especially toward the end of a dynasty, when society was in confusion, such men participated in armed uprisings, became their leaders, struck a blow at the authorities, and gave vent to their anger. Always visible behind the collapse of a dynasty were the schemes of such dissatisfied members of the intellectual class.

Following are some of the examples best known to history.

HUANG CH'AO. In the confused times of the late T'ang period, he was the leader of a great rebellion that almost destroyed the foundations of the dynasty. Born into a wealthy family in western Shantung, he studied hard and took the examinations but, because he failed repeatedly, abandoned hope for an official career, organized a secret society, and engaged in illicit dealings in salt, a government monopoly. Observing the disordered state of the empire, he raised an army and rebelled. His rebellion affected the whole country. After devastating the area from Kwangtung to the middle Yangtze valley in the south, he captured the capital, Ch'ang-an, massacred nobles and officials, and put himself upon the throne. But when the T'ang army returned the people rose against him, his organization collapsed, and many of his men surrendered to the T'ang. When he himself was killed, along with his family, the rebellion collapsed.

LI CHEN. Huang Ch'ao's subordinate Chu Chüan-chung rebelled against Huang Ch'ao, surrendered to the T'ang, and, after crushing the rebellion, seized power from the T'ang. Assisting and advising Chu was Li Chen, who had failed in the examination system. Deeply hating high court officials and aristocrats, especially nobles who had gone through the examinations, he killed thirty important officials of the declining dynasty and threw their corpses into the Yellow River. Chu Chüan-chung established himself as first emperor of the Later Liang (907–23), under whom Li was a powerful minister. When the Later Liang regime was destroyed and succeeded by the Later T'ang (923–34), Li Chen and his family were executed.

CHANG YÜAN-HAO. During the middle period of the Northern Sung, the Tanguts established the Hsi Hsia state (1038–1227) on the northwestern frontier and frequently hurt the Sung domains with their incursions. A traitor who assisted the Hsi Hsia, set up a Chinese-style court for them, introduced Chinese culture, and by acting as China's enemy caused the Sung much worry was Chang Yüan-hao, an educated man who had failed in the examinations.

NIU CHIN-HSING. The leader of a rebellion in Shensi during the late Ming period was Li Tzu-ch'eng, who went on to capture Peking and forced the last Ming emperor to commit suicide. Among the generals on Li's staff at that time were two graduates of provincial examinations. One of these was Niu Chin-hsing, who hated the Ming dynasty and everywhere hunted out and butchered members of the royal family and high officials. The other graduate was Li Yen, the son of a high Ming official, who advised Li Tzu-ch'eng that, in order to gain control of the empire, he must cease the senseless slaughter and win public support. When Li Tzu-ch'eng occupied Peking and put an end to the Ming dynasty, he held only military strength and did not enjoy the confidence of the people. In the end, having relied too much upon Niu Chin-hsing, Li Tzu-ch'eng was driven out of the capital by the Ch'ing forces, and perished soon after. It is worth noting that these two rebels held the status of graduates and that their inability to achieve the *chin-shih* degree drove them to support Li Tzu-ch'eng.

HUNG HSIU-CH'ÜAN. The leader of the mid-nineteenth-century Taiping Rebellion, which spread from the mountains of Kwangsi to the Yangtze delta, established its capital at Nanking, advanced north to threaten Tientsin, and shook the dynasty to its foundations, was the Kwangtung candidate Hung Hsiu-ch'üan, who had repeatedly failed to become a licentiate. Setting up a kind of transformed Christianity, he led his followers into a rebellion that left its mark upon sixteen of China's eighteen provinces. The Ch'ing government, with some assistance from foreign powers, barely managed to suppress the rebellion, but the dynasty's glory was shattered. It would not be wrong to say that this rebellion marked the beginning of the end of the Ch'ing dynasty.

Seen in this light, it is clear that the examination system not only produced officials loyal to a dynasty but also bred malcontents who opposed the central government and its emperor. The examination system was no exception to the general rule that all things have their positive and their negative aspects; and we must keep in mind the fact that dissatisfaction with the examination system was only one of many factors that led to the collapse of a dynasty. Indeed, when an old dynasty was replaced by a new, the latter undertook an early revival of the examination system practically unchanged. The fact that even the Kingdom of Heavenly Peace, which was established by the Taipings under the leadership of a failed licentiate, conducted a number of its own peculiar examinations shows better than anything else that governments found the examination system a most advantageous institution.

THE END OF THE EXAMINATION SYSTEM   To select officials by examinations is an idea that was not seriously considered in Europe until quite recently. There, deep-seated feudal ways remained influential, with the result that for a long time officials were selected according to birth or power, or else governmental posts went to the highest bidder under a primitive system of sale of office. England, where democracy was most advanced, did not reach the point of using examinations for government service until after 1870. In the United States of America this began in 1883. After that almost all countries followed suit. The case for Chinese influence upon the development of civil service examinations in Europe is strong. On the other hand, because China's system left education to the people, the country failed to keep pace with those of Europe. Public education in China reached its zenith about a thousand years ago, under the Sung dynasty, after which its story is one of unmitigated decline. During the Ming and Ch'ing dynasties, the university in the capital and the government schools in prefectures and districts were schools in name only, because no actual teaching took place in them. As a result China lagged in educational and therefore in social progress.

The inadequacy of the examinations themselves was frequently indicated by Chinese critics, who questioned whether memorizing the classics and writing poems and essays were really relevant to the tasks of government, charged that the system merely tested men's classical education, and asserted that the examination net failed to capture men who possessed genuine abilities and high moral character. Yet no alternative to the system was ever devised. Undeniably, outstanding men had come up through the examination system; and victory went to the common-sense view that, pointing to the system's achievements, upheld the status quo.

This was all very well as long as China remained powerful, the only strong country in East Asia. However, when East Asia began to feel the pressures arising from the new culture that arose in Europe with the Industrial Revolution, China was forced to change. To meet the new situation developing throughout the world, the acquisition of new knowledge and technology was necessary for every country. The only East Asian country that, perceiving this fact, adjusted quickly and successfully to the new times was Japan, where in 1872 the Meiji government proclaimed the establishment of a new educational system and philosophy that followed the European and American pattern. Japan's subsequent rapid economic and technological development owed much to this new educational system.

Chinese awareness of the need to acquire the new technology came after the nation suffered defeat in wars with European powers, and actually preceded the same realization in Japan. As early as 1866 a naval academy was founded in Fukien to train men for China's navy. Later, several institutes were established in different areas, all of which were called "academies," or *hsüeh-t'ang,* to distinguish them from the old-style schools, *hsüeh-hsiao.* Yet the outcome was not a general development of the new kind of education, because the old and deeply entrenched examination system blocked the diffusion of the new learning.

In 1901, after the bitter humiliation of the Boxer Rebellion and foreign intercession the preceding year, the Ch'ing government, at last realizing that change was essential, announced the establishment of a new school system for the entire country and concluded that this made necessary the abolition of the examination system. Many conservatives who had come up through the system raised strenuous opposition to this decision, but the general opinion favored the reformers' ideas. In the fifth month of 1904 the last examinations were held. When they ended the curtain was lowered forever upon an institution that had endured for more than thirteen hundred years.

When the examinations were abolished, the studies that had been required in order to prepare for them became completely useless. The men who had become graduates, or at least licentiates, were still relatively well off, since they had obtained respectable social status; but there were also older students who, not yet having reached that stage, still hoped to become licentiates. Since their minds were no longer flexible, they could not easily switch to the new learning. Too proud to turn to commerce, they were also too weak for physical labor. In a steadily changing world, their education and scholarship became more and more out of date, and in the end made them objects of ridicule. China was full of such failures. Lu Hsün, in his lively style, wrote a story depicting such a pathetic victim of the examination system or, more precisely, describing the marks it left upon Chinese society. Published fifteen years after the abolition of the examinations, the story is entitled "K'ung I-chi." These words comprise the second line in the children's primer (quoted on page 14, where they are translated as "Confucius himself"). They refer, of course, to the historical Confucius, but in time the phrase became the nickname for certain impecunious students. Here is the gist of the story:

The wineshop of Lü-chen, near Chinkiang, was filled with guests in short and long garments. The former were laborers, who, standing on the dirt floor, carried on boisterously while drinking their wine. The men in long gowns were high-class guests, for whom there was a separate room. Only one of them had joined the standing drinkers. He was tall, his greenish face scarred and his white beard unkempt, and his long gown looked as if it had not been mended or washed for more than ten years. Such was the student K'ung I-chi, who had been unable to become a licentiate. K'ung ordered a little heated wine and a side dish of aniseed, and started up a conversation with a young servant: "I know the character used in writing the name of this dish, and there are four ways to write its lower part. . . ."

Unable at times to meet his wine bill, K'ung, student though he was, sometimes stole or went shoplifting. The scars on his face were from wounds received on these forays.

The scene shifts to a time near the night of the harvest moon. For a long time the figure for nineteen cash, which K'ung had himself written on the shop's blackboard to acknowledge his debt, had remained unaltered. The autumn wind was blowing fiercely at this time of year, which gets colder with every day, when one afternoon K'ung entered the completely empty shop. A voice was heard ordering a bowl of warm wine, but K'ung was not visible from the counter. He could not be seen because his legs had been broken, and he had crawled into the shop. He had been discovered while trying to sneak into the house of a wealthy graduate, been beaten almost to death, and had his legs broken. His face was leaner and darker. His body was covered with tattered padded clothes, and suspended by a string from his shoulders was a sack on which he knelt. Supporting himself with both hands on the ground, he had made his way into the wine shop.

Excusing himself with a ridiculous "I turned and broke my legs," he paid four cash for the warmed wine, but the nineteen cash remained unpaid. Then he left. And that was all. K'ung was not seen again in the wineshop. Probably he died in some field.

THE EXAMINATION SYSTEM'S GREAT ACHIEVEMENT It is very easy to employ the standards of the present to criticize an institution that has already receded into the mists of history, but to do so would distort its significance. Furthermore, in developing our doubts about the examination system we must not simply follow the arguments that Chinese critics have offered but must consider the system in its relation to the society and the culture that allowed it to continue for so long. The fact that must be emphasized is that through the examination system the central government of China greatly favored literary studies and advanced civilians to important posts, while keeping subordinate to them the military officers with their concern for physical power. As we have seen, the military examinations were important only in theory and were neglected by the government and by society alike. The emphasis in the governmental examinations from the beginning was laid upon literary studies.

Before the Sung period there was no strict division between military and civilian officials, and, according to the ideal, a man could serve either as a minister or as a general, as the times required. But after the start of the Sung dynasty, the differences between them gradually increased. Officers up to the rank of unit commander were considered to be military officials and could rise no higher, since the posts of minister of war (*ping-pu shang-shu*) and chief of staff (*shu-mi shih*) were filled only by civilians. Furthermore, it was usual to assign civilians as front-line generals. The possibility that a military man could become a front-line commander and then go on to enter the central government as a minister of war or a chief of staff was most abhorrent to the Chinese, since it disrupted the entire concept of their political system. Consequently, they took precautions against such an event.

The policy of reserving those important positions for civilians, while restricting military men to posts no higher than that of unit commander, did have its drawbacks and did sometimes lead to dissatisfaction or even to tragedy. An example is provided by the fate of a Southern Sung patriot, Yüeh Fei (1104–42). During the long years of war against the Chin (Juchen), Yüeh Fei was an outstanding front-line unit commander and rose to the rank of general almost before anyone was aware of it. This rise of a military man made the court uneasy, so much so that, by various devices, Yüeh Fei ended as a victim of these fears and suffered a bitter death. Such an attitude damaged the efficacy of the military, since they concluded that it was foolish for a military man to try to distinguish himself. This policy of the government was not new at the time of Yüeh Fei, having been inherited from the Northern Sung.

The policy of restraining the power of military men invited trouble in times of war, but even so the idea of keeping centralized civilian control over the army, military affairs, and military command was an excellent one. The rule that no matter how great his accomplishments a professional military man could not participate in setting the government's policy at the highest levels may seem callous at first glance but is actually the foundation of good government, for if military men participate in government in their capacity as military men, they will emphasize the army's needs and will want to dominate the government as well as its foreign relations. It goes without saying that the military is necessary for the protection of the state, but for it to dominate the state is unbearable. As an English aphorism declares, "The army is the best servant, but the worst master." The speed with which an army deteriorates and becomes corrupt, once it has seized political power, has been demonstrated too frequently in history.

Among China's dynasties the Sung was especially firm in maintaining civilian control over the military, but the others also followed this general policy. Skipping the next dynasty, the Yüan, since it was established by the foreign Mongols, we come to the Ming, which, except for its initial period, maintained a policy of rule by civilians. The Ch'ing dynasty, too, even though it was founded dy the foreign Manchus, generally continued the policy of the Ming. The governors general and governors it appointed to supervise the military and civilian affairs of each province usually were civilians. Military men were appointed only in a few exceptional cases. All Chinese in the central government were civilians, as was the minister of war. Indeed, the appointment of a civilian to that post had been a matter of government policy from the time of the Sung.

Objections may be raised against the assertion that the history of China is a unified and peaceful one, marked by few wars, but we must not forget that China's size is comparable to that of all Europe. Frequently, at the beginning of China's successive dynasties, wars were necessary to pacify the interior and to conquer other states, but generally, after those conflicts came to an end, the vast nation was at peace. Especially during the Sung dynasty, when emphasis on civilian values reached a peak, there are few records of warfare, while during the same period in Europe, the late Middle Ages, there was a war somewhere or other almost every year—a record that we can say has continued to the present. Late in the Ch'ing dynasty, China suddenly became involved in a number of wars against foreign countries, but all of these conflicts were begun by other powers, not by China.

Military coups also were almost completely unknown in Sung and post-Sung China. Perhaps because a man who did attempt a coup could find no followers, nobody planned one to begin with. In any event, this shows that the people, or rather the intelligentsia and the wealthy people who formed public opinion, had reached a very high level of social responsibility. But, again, this is a comparative question; and if we ask at what stage in European history a class appeared that was comparable to the Sung intelligentsia, probably we would have to answer that it did not emerge before the Renaissance of the fifteenth and sixteenth centuries even in the most advanced European countries.

The examination system was based upon this class of Chinese intellectuals and flourished because of it. A *chin-shih* received his honorable status from the emperor, but at the same time his eminence was acknowledged by a public opinion formed and controlled by intellectuals. Otherwise, why would the examiners' every move, and the exact standing of those who passed the examinations, have been the main topics of conversation in society? We can say that the examinations had something of the character of elections; and we should note that the modern term for election, *hsüan-chü,* designated the examination system in imperial China. Earlier, the term had referred to the selection of popular men from the villages and their nomination to the central government, which thereupon, complying with public opinion, appointed them to office. Later, the emperor's autocratic power gradually increased, until appointment to office and the granting of the qualifications for office rested in his hands, and the new examination system was developed. Yet, in the Chinese view, this entrusting to the emperor of a function that once had belonged to the people was done for the sake of convenience, and the old term continued to be used for the selection of officials.

The *chin-shih,* qualified through the examination system and backed by public opinion, became China's statesmen and curbed the power of the army. This in itself was certainly a major accomplishment, for military intervention in national politics is always an unmanageable problem—even in some modern "advanced" countries.

SUGGESTIONS FOR FURTHER
READING

by Conrad Schirokauer

PROFESSOR MIYAZAKI'S TEXT implies the wide range of sources that can be made to yield insights into imperial China's examination system and reveals some of the most rewarding intellectual perspectives for understanding that system and the larger society of which it was an integral part. The purpose of this appendix is to assist those readers who wish to explore some of these matters in greater depth by suggesting where they might begin. The list of readings offered here is selective and introductory, but as far as possible it is up to date.

It is also uneven, because some of the most important and even obvious approaches to an understanding of the examination system still await serious and comprehensive analysis by modern Western scholars. Thus, since the work of Biot (1847) there has been no general history of education in China covering the period when the examinations flourished, although Grimm (1960) did analyze the Ming school system. One alternative to the inadequate government schools is indicated in the articles by Liu (1959) and Twitchett (1959), who point out the role of clan schools and the support given by clans to struggling takers of examinations. Biggerstaff (1961) and, more recently, Ayers (1971) have also included discussions of traditional Chinese education, although they are concerned primarily with attempts to adapt it to meet new, modern needs. Ayers, in addition, presents an interesting account of Chang Chih-tung's service as a director of studies (or director of education, to use Ayers's version of the title).

A beginning has been made, it is true, but even a cursory glance at any recent volume of the annual *Bibliography of Asian Studies* will show that, while numerous studies of Chinese education since 1949 have been published, no similar effort has been brought to bear on what came before that significant year.

A major concern of modern scholarship has been the study of imperial China's social structure and the question of social mobility. This has led to evaluation of the examination system in its role as a channel for upward mobility. As is indicated by the subtitle "Career Open to Talent?" this was a major subject for the collection of interpretative essays *The Chinese Civil Service*, edited by Menzel (1963)—which, incidentally, includes some well-considered suggestions for additional reading. The findings of Kracke and of Ho, both presented in that volume, showing that the examinations did provide a substantial infusion of new blood into the bureaucracy, do not contradict Miyazaki's picture of the intensity of the competition and the difficulty confronting the individual who sought to climb the "ladder of success."

In addition to presenting seven essays on social mobility, Menzel's book has a section called "Recruitment and the Struggle for Power," consisting of three items, and incorporates three others under the heading "The Attempt to Measure Talent." Among these is the important essay by Nivison (1960), which analyzes recurrent themes in Chinese critiques of the examinations. The books by Chan (1963) and Fung (1952, 1953) are recommended for those who seek a general understanding of the philosophical foundations of Chinese education and recruitment for government service; while Munro's more specialized philosophic investigation (1969) considers a theme basic to any thinking about education.

For the political dimensions and implications of the examination system, Menzel's volume adds theoretical statements from Max Weber and Karl Wittfogel, as well as the more empirical approach of Kracke (1957), which bring out some of the major issues lying behind political conflicts over the examinations. Wilhelm (1951), on the other hand, analyzes the imperial reasons for holding the "examination for great scholars" in 1679; and Meskill (1964) provides a description of the ceremonial conferring of the *chin-shih* degree upon successful candidates. Such studies of individual examinations are rare, unfortunately.

Important sources of information about the examinations are the biographies of men who took them. Outstanding among these is *The Life and Times of Po Chü-i*, by Arthur Waley (1949), still probably the best source in English on the examinations during the T'ang dynasty. Miyazaki has shown how rich Chinese literature is in examination lore, and how the lively details recounted in popular fiction can be used to augment drier, more official accounts. Included in this list of references are two of the works he quotes, *The Scholars*, by Wu Ching-tzu, and the stories of Lu Hsün, as well as the book by Liu Wu-chi (1966), a sensitive and well-written survey.

Some books have been listed primarily because they are basic sources for important times in the history of the examination system. Des Routours (1932) falls into this category as the major work on the T'ang period, while the book by Kracke (1953) is required reading for anyone who wants to understand the system as it functioned in the Sung period, which many people, including Miyazaki, regard as its high point. The two monographs by Zi (1894, 1896) are pioneering studies upon the Ch'ing period, replete with details. The work by Sun (1961) stands in a class by itself: its translations of Ch'ing official terminology are a splendid reference for the student of government, and have been followed whenever possible in this book. Franke (1960) presents a valuable discussion of the old system before giving an account of its abolition. For an explanation of the influence of the Chinese system upon the development of civil service examinations in countries in the West, Teng's article (1942–43) has been included in this list.

Finally, a few books of general orientation have been listed, such as the standard history by Reischauer and Fairbank (1958, 1965) and *Examinations* by Lauwerys and Scanlon (1969), cited in the introduction, which provides a sample of current professional thought upon examinations and information about their status and operation in a number of widely different modern countries.

For titles of other works referring to many topics raised in this book, the reader can best begin by turning to Chang Chun-shu's introductory bibliography (1971).

Association for Asian Studies. *Bibliography of Asian Studies*. Ann Arbor, Mich.: published annually.

Ayers, William. *Chang Chih-tung and Educational Reform in China*. Cambridge, Mass.: Harvard University Press, 1971.

Biggerstaff, Knight. *The Earliest Modern Government Schools in China*. Ithaca, N.Y.: Cornell University Press, 1961.

Biot, Edouard. *Essai sur l'histoire de l'instruction publique en Chine et de la corporation des lettres depuis les anciens temps jusqu'à nos jours*. Paris: B. Duprat, 1847.

Chan, Wing-tsit. *A Source Book in Chinese Philosophy*. 2 vols. Princeton, N.J.: Princeton University Press, 1963.

Chang Chung-li. *The Chinese Gentry: Studies on Their Role in Nineteenth Century Chinese Society*. Seattle, Wash.: University of Washington Press, 1955.

Chang Chun-shu. *Premodern China: A Bibliographical Introduction*. Michigan Papers in Chinese Studies, no. 11. Ann Arbor, Mich.: University of Michigan Center for Chinese Studies, 1971.

Chang, Richard T. Review of *Kakyo: Chūgoku no shiken jigoku* by Ichisada Miyazaki. *American Historical Review* 70 (1965): 1217.

Des Routours, Robert. *Le traité des examens traduit de la nouvelle histoire des T'ang*. Paris: Librairie Ernest Leroux, 1932.

Franke, Wolfgang. *Reform and Abolition of the Traditional Chinese Examination System*. Cambridge, Mass.: Harvard University Press, 1960.

Fung Yu-lan. *The History of Chinese Philosophy*. 2 vols. Translated by Derk Bodde. Princeton, N.J.: Princeton University Press, 1952–53.

Galt, Henry S. *History of Chinese Educational Institutions*. Vol. 1: To the Five Dynasties. London: Probsthain, 1951.

Grimm, Tilemann. *Erziehung und Politik im Konfuzianischen China der Ming Zeit (1368–1644)*. Hamburg: Mitteilungen der Gesellschaft für Natur und Völkerkunde Ostasiens 35 B, 1960.

Ho Ping-ti. *The Ladder of Success in Imperial China: Apects of Social Mobility (1368–1911)*. New York: John Wiley & Sons, 1962.

Kracke, Edward A., Jr. *Civil Service in Early Sung China*. Cambridge, Mass.: Harvard University Press, 1953.

———. "Family vs. Merit in the Chinese Civil Service Examinations during the Empire." *Harvard Journal of Asian Studies* 10 (1947):103–23. (Reprinted in part in Menzel, *The Chinese Civil Service.*)

———. "Region, Family, and the Individual in the Chinese Examination System." In *Chinese Thought and Institutions,* edited by John K. Fairbank. Chicago: University of Chicago Press, 1957. Reprinted in part in Menzel, *The Chinese Civil Service.*

Lai T'ien-ch'ang. *A Scholar in Imperial China.* Hong Kong: Kelly & Walsh, 1970.

Lauwerys, Joseph A., and David G. Scanlon. *Examinations—The World Year Book of Education.* London, 1969.

Liu Hui-chen Wang. "An Analysis of Chinese Clan Rules." In *Confucianism in Action,* edited by David S. Nivison and Arthur F. Wright. Stanford, Calif.: Stanford University Press, 1959.

Liu Wu-chi. *An Introduction to Chinese Literature.* Bloomington, Indiana: University of Indiana Press, 1966.

Lu Hsün (Chou Shu-jen). *Selected Works of Lu Hsün.* Peking: Foreign Language Press, 1956.

Menzel, Johanna M., ed. *The Chinese Civil Service: Career Open to Talent?* Boston: D. C. Heath & Co., 1963.

Meskill, John. "A Conferral of the Degree of *Chin-shih.*" *Monumenta Serica* 23 (1964):351–71.

Munro, Donald J. *The Concept of Man in Early China.* Stanford, Calif.: Stanford University Press, 1969.

Nivison, David S. "Protest against Conventions and Conventions of Protest." In *The Confucian Persuasion,* edited by Arthur F. Wright. Stanford, Calif.: Stanford University Press, 1960. Reprinted in Menzel, *The Chinese Civil Service.*

Purcell, Victor. *Problems of Chinese Education.* London: Kegan Paul, Trench & Trubner, 1936.

Reischauer, Edwin O., and John K. Fairbank. *A History of East Asian Civilization.* 2 vols. Boston: Houghton Mifflin, 1958, 1965.

Sun, Et-tu Zen. *Ch'ing Administrative Terms: A Translation of the Terminology of the Six Boards.* Cambridge, Mass.: Harvard University Press, 1961.

Teng Ssu-yü. "Chinese Influence on the Western Examination System." *Harvard Journal of Asian Studies* 7 (1942–43): 267–312.

Twitchett, Denis. "The Fan Clan's Charitable Estate, 1050–1760." In *Confucianism in Action,* edited by David S. Nivison and Arthur F. Wright. Stanford, Calif.: Stanford University Press, 1959.

Waley, Arthur. *The Life and Times of Po Chü-i.* London: George Allen & Unwin, 1949.

Wilhelm, Helmut. "The Po-hsüeh Hung-ju Examination of 1679." *Journal of the American Oriental Society* 71 (1951): 60–66.

Wu Ching-tzu. *The Scholars.* Translated by Yang Hsien-yi and Gladys Yang. Peking: Foreign Language Press, 1957.

Zi, Etienne. *Pratique des examens literaires en Chine. Variétés Sinologiques,* no. 5. Shanghai: 1894.

———. *Pratique des examens militaires en Chine. Variétés Sinologiques,* no. 9. Shanghai: 1896.

The following secondary studies are suggested for readers of Chinese and Japanese:

Araki Toshikazu 荒木敏一. *Sōdai kakyo seido kenkyū* 宋代科挙制度研究. Kyoto: Tōyō-shi kenkyū-kai, 1969.

Chu Pai-lien 朱沛蓮. *Ch'ing-tai ting-chia lu* 清代鼎甲錄. Taipei: Chung-hua shu-chü, 1968.

Miyazaki Ichisada 宮崎市定. *Kakyo* 科挙. Osaka: Akita-ya, 1946.

———. *Kyūhin kanjin no kenkyū* 九品官人の研究. Kyoto: Tōyō-shi kenkyū-kai, 1956.

Shang Yen-liu 商衍鎏. *Ch'ing-tai k'o-chü k'ao-shih shu-lu* 清代科舉考試述錄. Peking: San-lien shu-tien, 1958.

Teng Ssu-yü 登嗣禹. *Chung-kuo k'ao-shih chih-tu shih* 中國考試制度史. Nanking: Examination Yüan, 1936.

IMPORTANT EVENTS IN THE CHRONOLOGY
OF THE EXAMINATION SYSTEM

SUI: 581–618

587: Abolition of the nine-rank system and beginning of the examination system, including *hsiu-ts'ai, ming-ching,* and *chin-shih* examinations.

595: Fang Hsüan-ling, later a T'ang chief minister, receives his *chin-shih* at age eighteen.

T'ANG: 618–907

622: The first T'ang examination.

651: The *hsiu-ts'ai* degree is abolished.

875–84: The rebellion of Huang Ch'ao.

FIVE DYNASTIES: 907–60

908: The first examination conducted by the Later Liang (907–21). The examinations are continued despite the unrest during the Five Dynasties period.

NORTHERN SUNG: 960–1127 / SOUTHERN SUNG: 1127–1279 / LIAO (Khitan): 907–1125 / CHIN (Juchen): 1115–1234

960: The first Sung examination.

975: The first palace examination, thereafter a regular part of the examination system.

988: The first Liao examination.

992: The names of candidates are covered for the first time in the palace examination.

1007: The names of candidates are covered for the first time in the Board of Rites examination.

1015: Copies of answer sheets are prepared by clerks in the Board of Rites examination for the first time, and the practice of inspecting the copies is begun.

1057: Ou-yang Hsiu as examiner passes papers in the old literary style (*ku-wen*).

1067: Beginning of the practice of holding the examinations every three years.

1068: The new university law is established.

1069: The *ming-ching* degree in classical exegesis is abolished and the *chin-shih* alone is retained, but classical exegesis is added as an examination category for the latter.

1123: The first Chin examination.

1256: Wen T'ien-hsiang is first-place *chin-shih*.

YÜAN (Mongol): 1279–1368

1315: The first Yüan examination.

MING: 1368–1644

1370: The first Ming examination.

1466: Lo Lun is first-place *chin-shih*.

1481: Wang Hua, father of Wang Yang-ming, is first-place *chin-shih*.

CH'ING: 1644–1911

1646: The first Ch'ing examination.

1788: Decision to institute the reexamination of graduates and the metropolitan reexamination.

1853: The Taipings establish their capital at Nanking and hold examinations.

1858: Irregularities in the Chih-li (Hopei) provincial examination are discovered, and offenders are punished.

1901: Decision to change to a new educational system.

1904: The last examination under the old system.

REPUBLICAN: 1911–49

1919: Lu Hsün's "K'ung I-chi" is published.

GLOSSARY-INDEX

Fan Chung-yen, 95, 96

fang-shih ("teacher"; term used by provincial-examination graduates for assistant examiners), 56–57

fa-she (dropped from school with permission to return later), 35

feng-chih li-pu hui-shih ("Participant in the Board of Rites Metropolitan Examination Held by Imperial Decree"; banner inscription), 64

Five Classics (*Book of Poetry* [*Shih Ching*], *Book of Documents* [*Shu Ching*], *Book of Changes* [*I Ching*], *Book of Rites* [*Li Chi*], and *Spring and Autumn Annals* [*Ch'un-ch'iu*]): in education, 14–17; in district examination, 22, 24; in qualifying examination, 29; in "annual" examination, 35; in provincial examination, 50; in metropolitan examination, 67

Four Books (*Analects* [*Lun-yü*], *Great Learning* [*Ta Hsüeh*], *Doctrine of the Mean* [*Chung Yung*], and *Mencius* [*Meng Tzu*]): in education, 14–17; in district examination, 20, 21, 22; in qualifying examination, 27, 29; in "annual" examination, 35; in special preliminary examination, 38; in provincial examination, 45, 51; in metropolitan examination, 62, 72

fu (rhymed prose), 23, 101

fu-k'ang ta-ch'en (reexaminers of metropolitan-examination answers), 70

fu k'ao-kuan (deputy examiner): in provincial examination, 39–40; in metropolitan examination, 66

fu-pang (list of runners-up in provincial examination), 55

Fu Shan, 109

fu-sheng (secondary student; a category of licentiate), 34. *See also* licentiate

fu-shih. See prefectural examination

gifts and tips, 31, 32, 60

graduate (*chü-jen;* graduate of provincial examination), 56, 59–61; eminence of, 59–61

Great Learning (*Ta Hsüeh*), 16

guarantor: of family background, 19; of candidate's identity, 20, 27

han-ko hsiu-ts'ai. See apprentice scholar

Hanlin Academy (Hanlin *yüan*), 71, 100, 101, 108, 110, 120

Hanlin *yüan hsiu-chuan* (first-class compiler in Hanlin Academy), 100

Hanlin *yüan pien-hsiu* (second-class compiler in Hanlin Academy), 100

hao-chün (attendant), 44

hao-fang (examination cell), 41

hao-she (examination cell), 41

hao-t'ung (lanes in provincial-examination compound), 41, 44

hsiang-shih. See provincial examination

Hsien-feng (Ch'ing emperor; r. 1851–62), 62

hsien-shih. See district examination

Hsien-tsung (T'ang emperor; r. 806–21), 112

hsi-tzu lu ("caring for writing" incinerator), 63

Hsüan-tsung (T'ang emperor; r. 713–56), 112

hsüeh-cheng. See provincial director of studies

hsüeh-hsiao. See schools

hsüeh-t'ang (academies), 125

Hsüeh Yüan-ch'ao, 112

hsün-yao (instructor), 34

Huang Ch'ao, 122, 123

huang-pang ("imperial placard"; card bearing names of palace-examination graduates), 84

Huang Tsung-hsi, 109

Huang Yüeh, 47, 48

hui-k'uei (top sixteen metropolitan-examination graduates), 70

hui-shih. See metropolitan examination

hui-shih hei-chüan (printed copies of metropolitan-examination answers distributed by graduates), 71

hui-yüan (first-place metropolitan-examination graduate), 70

hu-ming (covering of candidates' names), 21

Hung Hsiu-ch'üan, 123

Imperial Rescripts on Education: *Sheng-lun Liu-yen*, 23; *Sheng-lun Kuang-hsün*, 23, 24, 25, 29, 35, 38

i-sheng. See apprentice scholar

Japan: influence of China on, 23; compared with China, 111; adoption of

The "weathermark" identifies this book as a production of John Weatherhill, Inc., publishers of fine books on Asia and the Pacific. Supervising editor, designer, and typographer: Suzanne Trumbull. Production supervisor: Yutaka Shimoji. Composition, printing, and binding: Samhwa Printing Co., Seoul. The typeface used is 11-point Monotype Baskerville, with Baskerville for display.